Other books in the
BIBLE STUDY TEXTBOOK SERIES

SACRED HISTORY AND GEOGRAPHY
ACTS MADE ACTUAL
ROMANS REALIZED
THE CHURCH IN THE BIBLE
ROMANS REALIZED
HELPS FROM HEBREWS

LOOKING EAST

EPHESUS.

(Agora), and the amphitheater.

THE

GLORIOUS CHURCH

A Study of Ephesians

BIBLE STUDY TEXTBOOK

THE
GLORIOUS CHURCH

A Study of Ephesians

by

Wilbur Fields

College Press, Joplin, Missouri

Copyright 1960

Wilbur Fields

Jacket by Daniel DeWelt

LITHOPRINTED IN THE UNITED STATES OF AMERICA BY
CUSHING - MALLOY, INC., ANN ARBOR, MICHIGAN, 1960

To

My Mother

THE GLORIOUS CHURCH
CONTENTS

INTRODUCTION

There are several features in this book that will make it helpful to you.

(1) *The entire text of Ephesians* is given in the American Standard Revised Version of 1901 A.R.V. This is a very accurate translation of the original Greek text.

(2) *Outlines and charts* on every chapter and many smaller sections are included. These will be very helpful in teaching the book and in studying it.

(3) *Numerous illustrations* are included that will help to make the message of Ephesians more vivid.

(4) *Over four hundred thought questions* on the text are given. By the aid of these questions, you should be able to think out the meaning of nearly every verse and important thought in the book. Most of these questions can be answered with no help except for the Bible itself.

(5) *A paraphrase of every verse is given.* These serve as a brief commentary, and show the connection of nearly every verse with the verses preceding it. Often reading the paraphrase alone will bring out the meaning of the verse in a vivid way.

(6) *The notes are brief and concise.* They are designed to help both the advanced student of the Bible, and the average church worker. There is a lot of ammunition for teaching and preaching.

(7) *There are 340 fact questions,* which are mainly prepared to check your knowledge of exactly what the text says.

The study of Ephesians will be very rewarding to you. This book will guide you to an understanding of the "glorious church" about which Paul wrote in Ephesians. It will be a means for our perfecting "unto the work of ministering, unto the building up of the body of Christ."

I. CAN YOU ANSWER THESE QUESTIONS?

1. Exactly what is it that is so wonderful about Christianity? (1:18; 3:17-18)
2. How can living people be *dead* in sins? (2:1)
3. What are the seven things upon which the Spirit has united the church? (4:4-6)
4. What are the duties of wives to husbands, and husbands to wives? (5:22-23)
5. How can a Christian stand against the tricks of the devil? (6:11)

These questions, and many others, will be answered in our study of Ephesians.

Ephesians is "one of the divinest compositions of man" (Coleridge).

Ephesians is a letter about heavenly things. (1:3, 20; 2:6; 3:10)

Ephesians has more to say about the church than any other New Testament epistle. See Chapter II, "The Glorious Church in Ephesians.") Ephesians has been called "The Letter About the Church." For this reason, this book is entitled *The Glorious Church*.

"The Ephesian converts publicly burned their books of magic, in value 50,000 pieces of silver (Acts 19:19). Truly, they were well recompensed when they received this letter, not to lead them into magic and sorcery, but into the mystery of Christ, and the hidden wisdom of God. They burned evil and superstitious volumes, and then obtained a letter which cannot be valued in silver and gold, an epistle of wonderful breadth and power, full of riches of the mind and the warm flow of a master spirit" (Fraser).

Fact Questions

1. Ephesians is described as a letter about what?
2. About what subject does Ephesians have more to say than any other New Testament epistle?

II. THE GLORIOUS CHURCH IN EPHESIANS

The church is the most precious institution on earth today. Ephesians has more to say about the church than any other New Testament letter. We need to picture the church in our minds as the glorious church described in Ephesians.

The word *church* occurs nine times in the letter (1:22; 3:10, 21; 5:23, 24, 25, 27, 29, 32). The term *body* (referring to the church) occurs nine more times (1:23; 2:16; 3:6; 4:4, 12, 16 (twice); 5:23, 30).

Consider the glorious church described in Ephesians:

1. *Christ loves her.* 5:23. Men may despise and belittle her, but Jesus Christ loves her.
2. *The church shall be presented to Christ.* 5:27. What will the people who are not in the church do then?
3. *God's wisdom is demonstrated by the church.* 3:10. If you are not in the church, God sent Christ to die all in vain, as far as you are concerned. You make God's mercy to appear to be foolishness.
4. *God is glorified in the church.* 3:20-21. Out in the world you cannot glorify Him.
5. *There is one body,* one church. 4:4. Because of the divisions among those who believe in Christ, the world does not believe that God sent Him. John 17:20-21. Pray to God that men will abandon their loyalty to denominations and sects and be members only of that glorious church to which God adds all saved people. Acts 2:47.
6. *Christ is the Head of the church.* 5:23; 1:22. Our opinion of the church will be just as high as our opinion of Christ.
7. *The church is the fullness of Christ.* 1:22-23. If we love Christ, we shall love the church, for it is filled by Christ.
8. *Christ is the Savior of the body.* 5:23. All saved people are members of the church. You cannot be saved and not be a member of the Lord's church.
9. *She shall be holy and without blemish.* 5:27. No man can excuse himself by saying, "There are too many hypocrites."
10. *The church is the beloved bride of Christ.* 5:31-32. Don't you want to be married to Jesus? And what will the Lord do to those who hate and hurt His bride?

III. EPHESUS

In Paul's time, Ephesus was religiously like Rome, and commercially like New York.

The city lay in the Roman province of Asia, on the west end of what is now Turkey, about three miles from the coast, near the mouth of the Cayster River. It stood on the sloping sides of two hills and in the river valley between them.

A little city grew on the site in ancient times. Legend said that the mother-goddess of the earth was born there. And there her temple was built. The temple was burned and rebuilt seven times during the centuries, each time on a grander scale. Rich King Croesus even helped build one of the temples. In 356 B.C., the night Alexander the Great was born, the temple burned. It was rebuilt to be one of the seven wonders of the world, and was there when Paul came to Ephesus.

The Cayster River valley extended far inland toward the east from Ephesus. It was connected by highways to the chief cities of the province. At Ephesus itself an artificial harbor was built, accessible even to the largest ships. Thus, Ephesus was the most accessible city of Asia, both from land and sea.

As ships came up the canal into Ephesus from the seacoast, the city could not be seen from a distance because of its position in the valley. But at a certain point, the city appeared, spread out before them, with its theater (seating 24,000) on the hillside and the temple of Diana on the lowlands.

Even in ancient times, however, engineers had trouble keeping the harbor and canal dredged of silt from the river.

Commerce flourished in Ephesus. Priscilla and Aquila may have left Corinth for Ephesus (Acts 18:1, 2, 26) because Ephesus was famous for the manufacture of luxurious tents and marquees, as well as to prepare the way for Paul's ministry there.

Paul's labors in Ephesus turned many of the Ephesians from Diana. A substantial church flourished there. Timothy and the apostle John (supposedly) preached there. In 262 A.D. when the temple of Diana burned again, the influence of Diana had so weakened that it was never rebuilt again. A church council was held there in 341 A.D. The city declined. Many of its stone buildings were in ruins, and the stone was used elsewhere, some even in St. Sophia's church in Constantinople.

The Turks captured the city in 1308, murdering its inhabitants, destroying its remaining buildings. The Cayster River, overflowing its banks, buried the site of Diana's temple and the low part of the city under many feet of silt. There is no city at all on the site of Ephesus today. A Turkish village named Seljuk is about a mile from the site. Most of the buildings of Seljuk are made of stone from the ruins of Ephesus.

A most interesting account of a modern visit to Ephesus can be found in H. V. Morton's *In the Steps of St. Paul.*

Fact Questions

3. Where is Ephesus located? By what river?
4. What religious legend helped the growth of Ephesus?
5. Why was Ephesus a most accessible city?
6. What is the status of modern Ephesus?

A Map Showing Ephesus and
Surrounding Territory

IV. DIANA OF THE EPHESIANS

At some time in the remote past the Assyrians or Babylonians in their vain imaginations conceived of a female deity, a mother goddess of the earth. They called her *Ishtar*. Other tribes and nations adopted the idea and borrowed some of the legends connected with her. But they often gave the goddess their own names and developed forms of worship and traditions of their own. Always, however, the worship was of man's own invention (not from God) and very vile. Her rituals included sacrifices and ceremonial prostitution.

The Cappadocians called her *Ma*, the Phoenicians, *Astarte,* the Phrygians, *Cybele*. In Egypt, she was *Isis;* in Asia (the province containing Ephesus) she was called *Diana*, or *Cybele*. The legend was started that she was born in the woods near Ephesus, and that there her image (of ebony wood) had fallen from the sky from Jupiter (also called *Jove* or *Dios*). Some speculate that originally she was a meteorite.

Later Ephesus fell to the Greeks, and the Greek and Asiatic civilizations blended. The Greeks believed in a virgin goddess called *Artemis,* the swift twin sister of Apollo, the goddess of chastity, the woods, and the hunt. The Greek name of *Artemis* was given to the dark Asiatic goddess. In fact, her name in the Greek New Testament is actually *Artemis*. Some of the Greek colonists in Asia represented the Ephesian Diana as Greek on their coins.

At first, the figures of Diana were crudely carved of wood. In later times, metal images were made, showing her with a headdress representing a fortified city wall. The upper part of her body was covered with breasts to show that she was the mother of all life. (However, Sir William Ramsay believed that these "breasts" actually represented the ova of bees. The bee was the symbol of Ephesus, and is found on most of its coins. The temple staff included a crowd of priests or "drones" who dressed like women. Also there was a crowd of priestesses known as *Melissai,* who represented the worker bees. The goddess was the queen bee.) The lower part of her body was wrapped up like an Egyptian mummy. Later images show her with stags or lions, possibly

15

because some associated her with the Greek goddess Artemis hunting. On most coins showing the goddess two lines run from her hands to the ground. These probably represent rods which were necessary to keep her in an erect position, because of her top-heavy shape.

The temple of Diana was one of the seven wonders of the ancient world. It was built on marshy ground, but uncommon pains were taken to give it a good foundation. It was 220 by 425 feet, with its roof supported on 107 pillars, each 60 feet high. It was nearly 220 years in the process of completion.

The temple of Diana was not only a place of worship, but a museum of the best statuary and painting. It owned valuable lands and controlled the fisheries. Its priests were the bankers of its enormous revenues. Because of its resources, the people stored money there for safe-keeping. It became to the ancient world practically all that the Federal Reserve system is to the United States.

An annual feast, called the *Artemisia*, attracted thousands of pilgrims to Ephesus from all parts of the world. No work was done for a month, while great crowds enjoyed a daily program of athletic games, plays, and sacrifices. Thousands of shrines of Diana were purchased by the visitors to take home as souvenirs or objects of veneration (Acts 19:24). These shrines were crude models of the temple with a female figure inside. They were made of clay, marble, or silver.

The worship of Diana may have contributed to the start of the worship of the Virgin Mary. It is a remarkable coincidence that one of the earliest churches in honor of Mary was built at Ephesus on the site of the famous temple of Diana, and that in that same city a synod (council) was held in 431 which first designated Mary as "Mother of God."

A frog pond now covers the site of Diana's temple, and a snowy water weed fills the pond. The site was discovered and excavated by J. T. Wood in 1870.

When we know something about dark Diana, we can better understand why Paul wrote to the Ephesians, "Walk not as the other Gentiles walk, in the vanity of their mind, having the understanding darkened, being alienated from the life of God through the ignorance that is in them, because of the blindness of their heart: Who being past feeling have given themselves over unto lasciviousness, to work all uncleanness with greediness. But ye have not so learned Christ" Eph. 4:17-20.

Fact Questions

7. What nationalities were the first to worship a Diana-type mother goddess?

8. What were the two legends about Diana's relationship to Ephesus?

9. Who was the Greek goddess that became associated with Diana?

10. Approximately how large was Diana's temple?

11. Describe the shrines of Diana that were sold.

12. Why might we think that the worship of Diana contributed to the start of the worship of Mary?

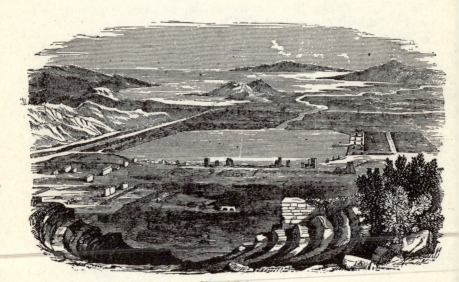

Site of Ephesus.

V. PAUL'S WORK AT EPHESUS
(Read all Scriptures)

1. *Brief visit* during the closing portion of his second missionary journey (A.D. 53) Acts 18:18-21.
2. *Main ministry in Ephesus*: (lasted three years, A.D. 54-57) Acts 20:31; 19:1-20:1.
   1. Paul baptizes twelve disciples. 19:1-7.
   2. Paul preaches three months in the synagogue. 19:8.
   3. Paul preaches in the school of Tyrannus. 19:9-10a.
   4. All Asia hears the word of God. 19:10b; cp. Rom. 16:5.
   5. Paul works special miracles. 19:11-12.
   6. The sons of Sceva fail to duplicate Paul's miracles. 19:13-17.
   7. Magic books are burned and the Word prevails. 19:18-20.
   8. I Corinthians and Galatians written at Ephesus.
   9. Paul sends Timothy and Erastus to Macedonia. 19:21-22.
   10. Demetrius stirs up the silversmiths against Paul. 19:23-28.
   11. Riot at the theater. 19:29-34.
   12. The town clerk quiets the riot. 19:35-41.
   13. Paul departs. 20:1.
3. *Farewell message to the Ephesian elders* (at Miletus). (A.D. 58, closing portion of the third missionary journey.) Acts 20:17-38.

   Paul was arrested at Jerusalem (A.D. 58) when Jews from Asia (Ephesus perhaps) falsely accused him. Acts 21:27-29.

Fact Questions

13. On what missionary journey did Paul first visit Ephesus?
14. How long did he remain there on that occasion?
15. On what missionary journey did Paul spend most of his time in Ephesus?
16. How long was Paul's main ministry in Ephesus?
17. What was the extent of Paul's success in Asia?
18. What writings did Paul write at Ephesus?
19. Who stirred up the riot against Paul in Ephesus?
20. At what place did Paul give his farewell message to the elders of Ephesus?

VI. VITAL FACTS ABOUT EPHESIANS

1. Who wrote Ephesians? Paul the apostle.
2. To whom was it sent?

(1) To the saints at Ephesus.
(2) To the faithful in Christ Jesus.
3. Where was it written? Rome.
4. When was it written? About A.D. 63, during Paul's first imprisonment.
5. Who delivered the letter? Tychicus (pronounced TICKY-kuss).

Evidently Tychicus delivered the epistle to the Colossians at the same time. Col. 4:7. He traveled with Onesimus (Oh-NESS-i-muss), whose master, Philemon (Fy-LEE-mon), lived at Colossae (Ko-LOSS-ee); see Colossians 4:7-9; Philemon 2. Onesimus bore the letter to his master Philemon.

Memory Work

Ephesians is a lofty letter, full of inspiration and grandeur. The entire epistle deserves to be memorized.

Passages that should by all means be committed to memory are 1:22-23; 2:8-10, 20; 3:10; 3:20-21; 4:4-6, 32; 5:25-27; 6:10-17.

Fact Questions

21. What was the date when Ephesians was written?
22. Who wrote Ephesians?
23. Where was Paul when he wrote it? What were his circumstances?
24. Who delivered the letter?
25. What other letters were dispatched at the same time?

VII. WAS EPHESIANS REALLY WRITTEN TO THE EPHESIANS?

There has been much discussion among scholars for many centuries over whether Ephesians was actually written to the Ephesians, or whether it was a circulating letter sent around to all the churches in the province of Asia.

Actually, the first verse of the letter answers the question. It was sent BOTH to the *saints which are at Ephesus* AND *to the faithful in Christ Jesus.* Obviously it was primarily and first sent to Ephesus, but was intended to be circulated around to the brethren elsewhere. This simple explanation clears up all the questions that have been raised about the matter.

There are practically no personal references in Ephesians, such as are common in Paul's other epistles. They are omitted

20

because those who read (or heard) the letter, but did not know Paul personally, would not be interested in the personal references. Those who did know Paul could find out from Tychicus all about Paul's affairs. In fact Tychicus was sent with the letter for that very purpose (Eph. 6:21-22).

It appears to us that the Epistle to the Ephesians was indeed first sent to Ephesus. Then a number of copies seem to have been prepared to be circulated around. In some of these copies the words *at Ephesus* (in 1:1) were omitted; conceivably the name of other cities could have been inserted.

Thus in the Vatican and Sinaitic manuscripts of the Bible (fourth century) and Papyrus 46 (third century) we do not find the words *at Ephesus* in 1:1. Basil (about 370 A.D.) tells us that the text without the words *at Ephesus* is "the way it was handed down to us by our predecessors, and so we ourselves have found it in the old copies." Origen (about 225 A.D.) wrote: "In the Ephesians alone, we find the expression, 'To the saints which are,' and we ask, unless the phrase *which are* is redundant, what can it mean?" It is most improbable that Paul would write *to the saints which are* without adding the name of some place. But thus the phrase stood in the copy seen by Origen.

However, when all the ancient manuscripts of Ephesians are checked, we find that the majority of them include the words *at Ephesus*. Also all of the ancient translations of the Bible (Latin, Syriac, etc.) have the words *at Ephesus,* and these translations must have been made from manuscripts older than any we now have. Furthermore, many of the Christian scholars of the first four centuries quoted from Ephesians, indicating that that was the title by which they were familiar with the epistle. Different people had simply seen different copies.

Some have speculated that the "epistle from Laodicea" (mentioned in Col. 4:16) may have been a copy of Ephesians. This can never be anything but a guess (and a very doubtful guess in our opinion). Tertullian (about 190 A.D.) said, "I say nothing here about another epistle which we have under the heading *to the Ephesians,* but the heretic (Marcion) *to the Laodiceans.* According to the true belief of the church we hold this epistle to have been dispatched to the Ephesians, not to the Laodiceans; but Marcion had to falsify its title, wishing to make himself out a very diligent investigator."
(International Standard Bible Encyclopedia).

Fact Questions

26. To what two groups of people is Ephesians addressed?
27. Why are there few personal references in Ephesians?
28. How can we account for the fact that some ancient manuscripts omit the words *at Ephesus* from 1:1?
29. Is the "epistle from Laodicea" (Col. 4:16) the same as Ephesians?

VIII.   DID PAUL WRITE EPHESIANS?

All the ancient manuscripts and versions of the Bible agree in stating that Paul wrote the Epistle to the Ephesians. All the Christian writers of the early centuries agree to this.

However, down through the years some critics have dared to assert that Paul did not write it. One recent doubter is F. W. Beare in the *Interpreter's Bible*. The arguments advanced by Mr. Beare against Paul's authorship are not arguments based upon external evidence. This is all in favor of Paul. They are based upon his own conceptions of what Paul believed and could have written or not written.

How could any man living in the twentieth century be better qualified to be a judge of what Paul could have written in the first century than the Christian scholars who lived in the centuries near to the time of Paul? These men had no doubts that Paul wrote Ephesians. Do we know Paul better than they? It is most unlikely.

To assert that Paul did not write Ephesians leads to some far-reaching conclusions. If Paul did not write it, it is a forgery, even if it be called a "pious forgery." A forgery is a form of lie. If, then, Ephesians contains a lie as to who wrote it, it cannot be inspired of God, for God cannot lie (Titus 1:2). If Ephesians is not inspired of God, it is only human wisdom, and is just as likely to contain untruths as any other book written by human wisdom alone. This we cannot accept for one second.

We are informed that there are 82 words found in Ephesians that are not found in any other of Paul's writings. This is supposed to prove that Paul could not have written Ephesians because it contains a vocabulary foreign to him. If this line of reasoning could prove that Paul did not write Ephesians, it would also prove that he did not write Romans (which has a hundred words not used by Paul elsewhere), or Colossians (which has thirty-eight). (Figures from Gerstner.) Paul used different words in Ephesians simply because he was writing about different subjects than he wrote about elsewhere.

It is also alleged that in several places (1:15; 3:2; 4:20-21) the "writer of Ephesians" indicated that he did not personally know those to whom he was writing, but had only "heard" of their faith. It is assumed that Paul, who had labored three years in and around Ephesus would have written as if he knew his readers intimately and not just by hearsay. But this objection has little weight. Paul had been away from Ephesus for six years when he wrote this letter. Any minister who has been absent from a field of his labor for six years would not write back to them and speak as if he personally knew all of them. Many changes and additions would have occurred in the membership during that time.

Furthermore, Paul wrote to Philemon, whom he knew well, indicating that he had heard of his faith and love (Phil. 5). The mere fact that Paul said he had *heard* of the faith of the Ephesians does not even suggest that he had never been with them.

The many similarities between Colossians and Ephesians have led some people to suggest that the "writer of Ephesians" borrowed freely from Paul's expressions in Colossians. Any person who has written several letters at the same time to different people knows how often one will use the same expressions in several letters. If the similarities between Colossians and Ephesians prove anything, they help to prove that Paul did write Ephesians at the same time he wrote Colossians.

Fact Questions

30. What external evidence could possibly indicate that Paul did not write Ephesians?

31. To what conclusions are we driven if Paul were not the actual author of Ephesians?

32. What does the fact that Ephesians has 82 words in it that are not used in Paul's other writings prove?

33. Does the fact that the writer says he had *heard* of the faith of the Ephesians prove that Paul did not write the epistle? Why or why not?

IX. OUTLINE OF EPHESIANS

Greeting; 1:1-2.
  I. DOCTRINES — Chapters 1, 2, 3.
   A. Blessings we have in Christ from God. 1:3-14.
   B. Paul's prayer for our enlightenment. 1:15-23.
   C. Once dead, now alive with Christ. 2:1-10.
   D. Once aliens, now fellow-citizens with the saints. 2:11-22.
   E. Paul's prayer for our strengthening. 3:1, 14-19.
      Parenthetical discussion of Paul's ministry. 3:2-13.
   F. Doxology. 3:20-21.
 II. DUTIES — Chapters 4, 5, 6.
   A. Keep the unity of the Spirit. 4:1-16.
   B. Walk as becometh saints. 4:17-5:20.
   C. Subject yourselves one to another. 5:21-6:9.
      1. Wives and husbands. 5:22-33.
      2. Children and fathers. 6:1-4.
      3. Slaves and masters. 6:5-9.
   D. Put on the whole armor of God. 6:10-20.
Conclusion. 6:21-24.
   A. Tychicus sent. 6:21-22.
   B. Benediction. 6:23-24.
(More detailed outlines precede the notes on each section.)

Fact Questions

34. What are the two main divisions of Ephesians, and what are their Scripture limitations?

35. Name the six topics in the first half of Ephesians, and tell which chapter each is in.

Diana.

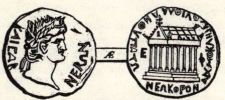

Coin of Ephesus, exhibiting the head of Nero and the Temple of Diana.

The same word, *neokoros,* is used on this coin to describe Ephesus as is used in Acts 19:35, where it is translated (in A. R. V.) "temple keeper".

EPHESIANS ONE

We can well call this chapter the "blessing chapter" of the Bible.

In this chapter there are MANY wonderful answers to the question, "Exactly what is so wonderful about Christianity?"

Previewing in Outline Form (1:1-14)

Greeting; 1:1-2.
1. By Paul. 1:1.
2. To the saints at Ephesus.
3. To the faithful in Christ Jesus.
4. Grace and peace requested for them. 1:2.

A. Blessing we have in Christ from God. 1:3-14.
1. God blessed for bestowing spiritual blessings. 1:3.
2. Blessings listed. 1:4-14.
   a. He chose us in Christ. 1:4.
      (1) Chosen before the foundation of the world.
      (2) Chosen to be holy and without blemish.
   b. He foreordained us unto adoption as sons. 1:5-6a.
      (1) Done according to His good pleasure.
      (2) For the praise of the glory of His grace. 1:6a.
   c. He bestowed grace (favor) upon us. 1:6, 8.
      (1) Bestowed upon us in Christ, the Beloved.
      (2) Grace made to abound in wisdom and prudence. 1:8.
   d. We have redemption in Christ. 1:7.
      (1) Through Christ's blood.
      (2) Redemption is the forgiveness of our trespasses.
   e. He made known to us the mystery of His will. 1:9-10.
      (1) Made known according to the good pleasure which He purposed in Christ. 1:9.
      (2) Made known unto a dispensation of the fulness of times. 1:10.
   f. In Christ we are made a heritage. 1:11-12.
      (1) Having been foreordained according to the purpose of God. 1:11.
      (2) That we be unto the praise of His glory. 1:12.
   g. In Christ we were sealed with the Holy Spirit. 1:13-14.
      (1) Sealing follows hearing the Word. 1:13.

26

(2)   Sealing follows believing the Word.
(3)   The Holy Spirit is an earnest of our inheritance. 1:14.

Text (1:1, 2)

Paul, an apostle of Christ Jesus through the will of God, to the saints that are at Ephesus, and the faithful in Christ Jesus: 2 Grace to you and peace from God our Father and the Lord Jesus Christ.

Thought Questions (1:1-2)

1. What does Paul imply by saying that he was an apostle *through the will of God?*
2. This letter is addressed to the *saints.* Are all Christians saints? Is there any distinction between the *saints* and *the faithful* who are mentioned in the next phrase?
3. What do you think that *grace* is? Look up the meaning of this word in a dictionary. Why do we need grace?

Paraphrase

1. Paul, an apostle of Christ Jesus through the will of God (and not of man), to the holy ones (the saints) that are in the city of Ephesus, and to the faithful souls in Christ Jesus elsewhere,
2. May divine favor and peace be given unto you from God our Father, and from the Lord Jesus Christ, through Whom the Father dispenses His blessings.

Notes (1:1-2)

1. Paul, who wrote this letter (see Introduction, section VIII), was an apostle through the will of God. He was no imposter. His life history, his power to work miracles, and his complete dedication to Christ all prove that he was a true apostle. See Galatians, chapters 1 and 2, for Paul's defence of his apostleship.
2. Paul addressed the brethren at Ephesus as *saints.* All Christains are saints. The word *saint* means *a holy* one. All Christians must be holy. I Pet. 1:16.
3. Notice that the letter is addressed to the saints at Ephesus, and to the faithful (or believing ones) in Christ Jesus. We understand that this epistle was sent to Christians in other places as well as to those in Ephesus. (See Introduction, section VII.)

4. Grace is God's undeserved favor. The teaching that we are saved by God's favor, and not because we deserve it, is a central doctrine in Ephesians and throughout the New Testament.
5. Grace and peace were meaningful wishes for the saints in an age of wholesale massacres of the saints by Caesar.

Fact Questions

36. Through what was Paul an apostle?
37. What are *saints?*
38. To what two groups is the epistle addressed?
39. What two things did Paul wish for the Ephesians?
40. What is *grace?*
41. From Whom do grace and peace come?

Thought Questions (1:3-14)

4. Count how many times the text says (in 1:3-14) that our blessings are given "through Christ," or "in Christ," or "in Him" (Christ), or uses other such phrases referring to Christ. What does this indicate to you about the need for Christ? (Note: Such phrases as *in Christ* occur 164 times in the writings of Paul.)
5. Count how many times such phrases as *to the praise of His glory* occur in 1:3-14. What does this indicate to you about the necessity for praising God?

Notes (1:3-14)

Note the purposes of the blessings as stated in the text:

(1) *That we should be holy and without blemish* (blame) *before God.* 1:4; 5:27. God wants us to be in His presence in heaven forever. But He does not want people there whose lives are spotted, blemished, and unclean with sin. His goodness in giving us these blessings should cause us to repent of sins (Romans 2:4).

(2) *That we should be "to the praise of his glory."* (1:6, 12, 14). We must, therefore, praise God with psalms, songs, testimonies, and prayers. Heaven will be a place of perpetual praise. If we do not praise God, we disappoint God and resist His purpose in giving us the blessings.

(3) *That he might gather together in one all things in Christ, both the things that are in heaven and that are on earth;* 1:10. Sin has broken up and disunited mankind, and also the angels in heaven (Jude 6). But now through Christ, God is

28

working toward an age (dispensation) when He shall bring together again for Himself one great harmonious universe in Christ. Sinners shall be cast out, but all who will receive the blessings shall be saved, and gathered into one great fellowship in Christ. Don't you want to be a part of that one great body that will be gathered together in Christ?

Fact Questions

42. Name the three purposes for which God has blessed us.

Text (1:3)

3 Blessed *be* the God and Father of our Lord Jesus Christ, who hath blessed us with every spiritual blessing in the heavenly *places* in Christ

Thought Questions (1:3)

6. What is the reason for which Paul blessed God in this verse?
7. Can Christ be equal with God, and yet call God His God?
8. What kind of blessings are spiritual blessings? Are there no material blessings attached to the gospel of Christ?
9. What are the *heavenly places?* Does this refer to heaven? or to the church? or to both? or to something else?
10. In Whom are these blessings bestowed?

Paraphrase

3. Praised be the God and Father of our Lord Jesus Christ, who with every spiritual blessing has blessed all of us who are in the heavenly places in Christ, namely in the church.

Notes (1:3)

1. Truly the Father God deserves to be blessed and praised for blessing us with every spiritual blessing. Of course, we know that He has blessings beyond measure yet in store for His saints in the life to come.

2. The Ephesians doubtless felt that they were more highly blessed than any other people, because the great image of Diana was in their city (bringing great wealth with it). God wanted the Christians to know that His blessings came *through Jesus Christ,* not Diana (or even the law of Moses). For that reason, God inspired Paul to write this section. Any one of these blessings is enough to make Christianity wonderful. But Christians have ALL of these blessings.

3. By a relationship too deep for human understanding, Christ is said to be equal with God (Phil. 2:6; John 5:23), and yet to honor God, the Father, as His God (Eph. 1:17; John 20:17).

4. The Law of Moses promised many material blessings (Deut. 7:12-16). The gospel contains some material promises (Matt. 6:33; Phil. 4:19), but its promises are mainly spiritual. Therefore the appeal of the gospel is not to the carnally minded, but to those who seek the abiding things of the Spirit (II Cor. 4:18).

5. The word *places* in the phrase *heavenly places* is not in the original Greek text. (Therefore it is written in italics in our text.) The expression is just *the heavenlies.*

    The term *heavenly places* refers to Heaven itself in Eph. 1:20. In Eph. 3:10 and 6:12 it seems to refer to the region of the air, the atmospheric heavens.

    However, here in 1:3 and in 2:6, it seems to refer plainly to Christ's church. This glorious institution is certainly a heavenly place. In the church our citizenship is in Heaven. Phil. 3:20. The church is called "the Kingdom of Heaven" often in the parables of Christ.

    If we say that the *heavenly places* in this verse (1:3) refer to Heaven itself, we will also have to say that God has no more spiritual blessings in Heaven than what he has given to us. (For God hath blessed us with every spiritual blessing in the heavenly places.) Anyone will admit that God has some spiritual blessings he has not yet given to us. Therefore we have to interpret the phrase *heavenly places* as referring to the church, in which God has blessed us with all of these spiritual blessings.

Fact Questions

43. What is the title of the section (1:3-14) in the outline?
44. Who is praised (or blessed) in 1:3?
45. Why is He blessed?
46. What kind of blessings are given?
47. In what places are the blessings given?
48. What does the phrase *heavenly places* refer to? Give reasons for your answer.
49. Through Whom (or in Whom) do the blessings come?

Text (1:4-6)

4 even as he chose us in him before the foundation of the world, that we should be holy and without blemish before him: in love 5 having foreordained us unto adoption as sons through Jesus Christ unto himself, according to the good pleasure of his will, 6 to the praise of the glory of his grace, which he freely bestowed on us in the Beloved

Thought Questions (1:4-6)

11. In Whom did God choose us? When did God make this choice? Did God choose us as individuals, or as a class of people? Exactly what did God choose concerning us?

12. The Jews had the adoption in Old Testament times (Rom. 9:4; Ex. 4:22). Who has that honor now?

13. Did God choose us to be before Him in love? Or, did He in love foreordain us unto adoption as sons? Either reading is possible. Which seems better to you?

14. What does *foreordain* (or *predestinate*) mean?

15. Did God foreordain us because we deserve it, or according to some other reason? Read the text (v. 5) carefully to see.

16. What purpose did God have in mind for choosing and foreordaining us? (v. 6)

17. Who is the Beloved? See Matthew 3:17. What did God freely bestow upon us in the Beloved?

Paraphrase

4. God has truly blessed us with every spiritual blessing, even as He, before the world was created, chose us who are in Christ to be in His presence holy and without blemish,

5. having in love foreordained that we should be adopted as sons unto Himself through Jesus Christ, and this He did according to the benevolence of His own disposition towards men of all nations,

6. in order that praise might be given unto Him for that glorious display of His grace, which He has so graciously bestowed upon us through Christ the Beloved one. (Eph. 2:7.)

Notes (1:4-6)

1. Long ago, even before God created the world, God decided, "The people who accept My son Jesus Christ shall be My chosen people." God did not choose certain individuals to go to heaven and others to go to hell. "Whosoever will" may ac-

31

cept Christ (Rev. 22:17). But God chose a class of people. He chose those who are in Christ to be His people.

2. Our being holy and without blemish is the consequence of being chosen, and not the condition of it. We cannot say to God, "I am holy and without blemish. You have to choose me as one of your people." Rather, God says to us, "You are sinners. But I have chosen you because you have accepted Christ. Now be ye holy and without blemish."

3. As sinful as we have been, it would be a favor to us if God permitted us to scrub the floors of heaven. But God, in love, honors us by adopting us as His children. What more could God do for us?

4. We prefer to put the phrase *in love* with the words that follow it. *In love* is an unnecessary additional description of us if we are holy and without blemish before the Lord. But it makes good sense to think that God has "in love" foreordained us to be adopted as sons unto Himself. There is no other reason why God would have decided to do such a great thing for us, if it were not done *in love*.

Back before the world existed, God said something to this effect: "I do make this decision and law now, even before man is created, that those who accept My son Jesus will be My chosen people, and they shall receive adoption as My children."

5. We have listed *hath chosen* and *having predestinated us* as separate blessings in the outline. The expression *having predestinated (foreordained) us* may be subordinate to *chosen* in v. 4. The choosing and foreordaining were acts done at the same time, and are closely related to each other. But still, they were separate decisions and plans made by God. Therefore, we have listed them separately in the outline.

6. The expression *freely bestowed* (v. 6) comes from the same root as the word *grace*. Rotherham's translation of v. 6 brings this out very clearly: "Unto the praise of the glory of His *favour* (grace), wherewith he *favoured* us in the Beloved One." The expression means *to pursue with grace, compass with favor, honor with blessings*. The King James translation of v. 6 is not good.

7. The idea of being saved by GRACE (favor) is completely strange to most people in our self-righteous age. They do not consider themselves to be sinners. Therefore, they do not feel that they need grace to be saved. They protest the treatment

they get from the world around them, but not one in fifty seems to have the slightest consciousness of sin. But true Christians will be conscious of their sinfulness, and praise God for the glory of His grace.

Fact Questions

50. Who did God choose to be His people?
51. When was the choice made?
52. What two characteristics did God desire us to have when we are before Him?
53. Unto what did God foreordain those who are in Christ?

Text (1:7, 8)

7 in whom we have our redemption through his blood, the forgiveness of our trespasses, according to the riches of his grace, 8 which he made to abound toward us in all wisdom and prudence,

Thought Questions (1:7-8)

18. What is *redemption?* From whom or from what are we redeemed?
19. What is the relationship of redemption to the forgiveness of our trespasses?
20. How freely has God dispensed His grace toward us? (v. 8)
21. What is the value of God granting grace to us in *wisdom and prudence?*

Paraphrase

7. In Whom (Christ) we have the ransom through His blood, namely the forgiveness of our sins. This redemption is provided unto us according to the wealth of His favor,
8. that favor of which He has poured out in abundance (even super-abundance) unto us, but in so doing has always bestowed it with all wisdom and understanding.

Notes (1:7-8)

1. Thank God for the blood of Christ. To those who understand its power and the need for it, it is the most valuable thing in the universe.

    "Many persons have a great objection to the word 'blood,' and I have a great objection to those persons. If we take out the blood of Christ, we leave the New Testament without a theme and without a purpose." (Joseph Parker)

33

2. *Redemption* is a releasing effected by the payment of a ransom. This idea is also an offence to many. Nevertheless, the truth remains that when we sin, divine, immutable justice is offended. The just law of God condemns us to death. Some payment must be made, or the sinner will perish.

   The blood of Christ washes away sins. When this takes place, the Law of God has no more claim against us. Thus we are redeemed from the just claims of the Law of God against a guilty soul. God does not pay the redemption price to the Devil. All souls belong to God, even the souls of sinners, and God alone judges and sentences them.

3. The forgiveness of sins (in 1:8) refers to the same thing as redemption, except that in the case of *redemption* our helpless condition in sin is primarily in view, whereas in the term *forgiveness* our own personal responsibility and guilt is thrust forth for us to behold and at which to shudder.

4. We obtain this redemption at our conversion, and it is available unto us every day thereafter.

5. God has showered grace upon us so freely that it *abounds*. There is almost more grace than there is power to use it. But in all things, God bestows His grace with prudence and understanding, so that it will do the most good.

Fact Questions

54. What does the word *redemption* mean?
55. What is the relationship between redemption and forgiveness of sins?
56. To what degree has God extended grace toward us?
57. With what two good provisions has God regulated the way He gives grace to us?

Text (1:9, 10)

9 making known unto us the mystery of his will, according to his good pleasure which he purposed in him 10 unto a dispensation of the fulness of the times, to sum up all things in Christ, the things in the heavens, and the things upon the earth;

Thought Questions (1:9-10)

22. Why would God's will be called a *mystery?* We are told in II Cor. 11:3 that there is simplicity in Christ. How can the gospel of Christ be a thing of simplicity, and a mystery too?

34

23. What is a *dispensation?* Do some research on the meaning of this word.

24. What age or time is the *dispensation of the fulness of times?* Could this be the present Christian dispensation?

25. What does it mean *to sum up all things in Christ?* Does this teach that everyone will eventually be saved?

26. What do you think *the things in heaven* are? Is Christ the head over heavenly beings, as well as redeemed humans?

Paraphrase

9. God has made grace to abound toward us, having made known unto us (the apostles) the "sacred secret" (Rotherham translation) of His will, in a manner according to His benevolent pleasure which He purposed within Himself;

10. And this mystery He did make known in order to bring all things unto a dispensation (administration) of the fulness of the times, in which dispensation He now plans to bring all beings hitherto disunited by sin under one head in Christ, both the things in heaven and the things upon the earth.

Notes (1:9-10)

1. *Having made known* (King James Version) is a more accurate translation than *making known,* given in the American Revised Version. Christ made known all truth to the apostles. He is not making known additional truths to anyone.

2. In the New Testament the word *mystery* is often used to refer to some hidden or unrevealed information which God has now made known. One of these mysteries was God's plan of salvation for men through Christ. This plan was once hidden, but it is now revealed. You might say it is not a mystery any longer. But it was an unrevealed mystery for many ages. (See Ephesians 3:3-6.)

3. Down through all the ages men have invented all kinds of religions and philosophies in an effort to discover what is really the truth. God's final truth was not revealed until Christ made it known. Previous to that time men could only guess about His law and promises. But now the mystery has been cleared up. We ought to thank God for making known this mystery of His will.

4. When God planned out His purpose and program for the ages, He planned toward a dispensation of the fulness of the

times, when all things would be summed up in Christ. We are thankful that God is now working out this purpose in all human affairs.

5. This *dispensation of the fulness of the times* obviously refers to our present Christian age. For it is during this age that God is endeavoring to bring all things under the headship of Christ.

6. To *sum up* means to gather under one head or to sum up as one might sum up the main points of a speech in a few statements. What a glorious universe this will be when all things are under the headship of Christ.

7. Verse 10 does not teach that eventually all men, angels, and other creatures will be saved. Paul plainly teaches in this letter that sinners will perish. (See 5:5-6.) Sinners will be cast out, and then Christ shall be head over all.

8. We surely do not fully grasp the great meaning in the words *the things in the heavens and the things upon the earth*. We do know that Christ is Lord of angels as well as of men (I Pet. 3.22). He is Lord of the dead as well as of the living. But God's plans for the whole universe are all designed to glorify Christ.

Fact Questions

58. What has God made known to us through Christ?
59. Why is God's will called a *mystery?*
60. What purpose does God have in mind for our sin-disunited universe?

Text (1:11, 12)

in him, *I say*, 11 in whom also we were made a heritage, having been foreordained according to the purpose of him who worketh all things after the counsel of his will: 12 to the end that we should be unto the praise of his glory, we who had before hoped in Christ:

Thought Questions (1:11-12)

27. What is a *heritage?*
28. Who or what is God's heritage at the present time?
29. Whose plan was it that we would be a heritage?
30. What people are those *who had before hoped in Christ?*

36

Paraphrase

11. In Whom (Christ) we Jews, as well as you Gentiles, were made a heritage, a private possession for God, having been foreordained to this honor not by virtue of Abrahamic descent and the law, but according to that pre-planned program which God, who does all thing according to the counsel of His will, laid out in Christ;

12. In foreordaining us to be His heritage, God was working toward the purpose that we would be a people devoted to praising His glory, we, the Jews, who in ages before have been the first to have hoped in the Messiah (or Christ).

Notes (1:11-12)

1. The *we* of v. 12 refers to Jewish Christians such as Paul. The *ye* of vs. 13 refers to Gentile believers, like most of the Ephesians. For centuries the Jews had been told of the coming of the Messiah (or Christ), and had hoped in Him. The Gentiles for the most part never heard of the Messiah until after the church was established on the day of Pentecost Acts 2), indeed not until after the conversion of Cornelius (Acts 10).

2. The reading of 1:11 in the King James Version, "We have obtained an inheritance," is not a good translation. The American Revised Version is correct here. It is true that we have obtained an inheritance. But we shall not fully receive it in this life. (See I Pet. 1:4.)

3. A *heritage* is a possession that one owns by right of inheritance. In the ages before Jesus came, the Jewish people were God's portion, His heritage. (See Joel 3:2; Ex. 4:22.) But now God has broken this arrangement with the Jews, and Christians have become His heritage. This was no afterthought, but was God's plan and purpose from the beginning. The Jew had come to feel that it was his particular privilege to be God's heritage; but God had not so foreordained it from the beginning. God had foreordained that the Jew would be a part of His heritage along with the Gentiles when both were in Christ.

4. The people of Old Testament times certainly offered much praise to God. But it is noteworthy that the Jews were made to be God's heritage IN CHRIST, so that they would be unto the praise of His glory. We cannot really praise God unless that praise is offered in Christ.

5. Concerning the *purpose* of 1:11 (and see also 3:11): God's workings are not the result of chance or impulse. Before time began God laid out in His mind a program (*prothesis,* or purpose) for the ages. Christ was at the heart of this program. We who are in Christ can thank God that we are the ones who are called according to His *purpose.* (See Romans 8:28.)

Fact Questions

61. What have we been made to be for God? (1:11)
62. When did God decide that those who are in Christ would be His heritage?
63. For what purpose were we foreordained to be God's heritage?
64. Who are the *we* who had before hoped in Christ?
65. According to what were we foreordained and made a heritage?

Text (1:13, 14)

13 in whom ye also, having heard the word of the truth, the gospel of your salvation, — in whom, having also believed, ye were sealed with the Holy Spirit of promise, 14 which is an earnest of our inheritance, unto the redemption of *God's* own possession, unto the praise of his glory.

Thought Questions (1:13-14)

31. What people are addressed as *ye also* in v. 13? With whom are they contrasted? (See v. 12.)
32. What two things does Paul say had been done before the Ephesians were sealed with the Holy Spirit? Does this indicate that they were saved as infants?
33. What is an *earnest?* The dictionary will give you a good definition of this term.
34. What is the *earnest of our inheritance?* Why is this a most appropriate and befitting earnest?
35. What does *ye were sealed* mean? How is a document sealed? Why? How are we sealed with the Holy Spirit?

36. If we already have redemption (v. 7), why must we be satis-
    fied with an earnest unto (or until) the redemption? Are
    there two meanings of the word *redemption?* If so, what
    does it mean here? (Compare Rom. 8:18-23.)

37. What (or who) is God's own possession?

Paraphrase

13. In Whom (Christ) you Gentiles also, having first heard the
    word of truth, the gospel of your salvation, and having also
    believed in Christ, were stamped and sealed as being God's
    own possession with the Holy Spirit which was promised
    unto us.

14. The Holy Spirit is the earnest, the advanced portion, of our
    inheritance; and we shall enjoy this earnest of the Spirit
    until the redemption of God's possession, i.e., until the time
    when the people who are God's own through Christ are raised
    from the dead unto eternal life, and all this shall redound to
    the praise of His glory as Saviour.

Notes (1:13-14)

1. Official papers are often stamped with a seal. This seal proves
   that the document is approved by the proper authorities.
   Seals have been used since ancient times. Cylinder-shaped
   seals, or seals carved on rings were used to make official im-
   pressions on clay tablets.

   When we (1) heard the Word of truth, the gospel, and
   (2) believed it (and, of course, were baptized; Gal. 3:26-27),
   God gave us the gift of the Holy Spirit (Acts 2:38). The
   Holy Spirit produces in us holiness and many good fruits.
   (See Gal. 5:22-23.) Thus the Holy Spirit in the Christian
   stamps and seals him as being "God's property." It ought
   to be obvious to anyone who associates with a Christian that
   he is *sealed* with God's Spirit.

2. The Holy Spirit is an *earnest* of our inheritance until the
   complete redemption of the purchased possession. An *ear-*

39

nest is money which is given when a bargain is made, as a pledge that the full price will be paid later. Right now we Christians have the earnest of the Holy Spirit. This brings to us love, joy, peace, etc. These joys are an earnest of the boundless joys we shall have when Jesus comes back, and the dead are raised, and sin is destroyed forever. The joy we have as Christians now is only a sampling of the greater joys in store for us.

3. The *Holy Spirit of promise* means the *promised Spirit* (Zech. 12:10; Isa. 32:15).

4. The *redemption* of 1:7 refers to our redemption from sin. The *redemption* here in 1:14 refers to our redemption from human frailty and from the curse. (See Genesis 3:17-19.) This will occur when our bodies are raised from the grave. (See I Cor. 15:43-44, 51-55.)

Fact Questions

66. What two acts did Paul say had been done before *ye were sealed?*

67. With what are we sealed?

68. What is the *earnest* of our inheritance?

69. How does the Holy Spirit serve as an earnest of our inheritance?

70. What is the redemption referred to in 1:14?

EPHESIANS ONE

"The Blessing Chapter"

GREETING — 1:1-2

BLESSINGS WE HAVE IN CHRIST — 1:3-14

1. Chosen — 4
2. Foreordained To Adoption — 5
3. Grace Bestowed — 6
4. Redemption — 7
5. God's Will Revealed — 9
6. Inheritance — 11
7. Sealed With The Spirit — 13-14

PRAYER THAT WE BE ENLIGHTENED ABOUT OUR BLESSINGS — 1:15-23

Previewing in Outline Form (1:15-23)

B. Paul's prayer for his readers' enlightenment. 1:15-23.
  1. Basis of the prayer. 1:15.
    a. The blessings of 1:3-14.
    b. Having heard of the Ephesians' faith.
    c. Having heard of their love toward the saints.
  2. Thanks given always. 1:16.
  3. Requests. 1:17-23.
    a. That God would give them a spirit of wisdom and revelation. 1:17-18a.
      1) Based in the knowledge of Himself. 1:17b.
      2) Having the eyes of your heart enlightened. 1:18a.
    b. That they would know these things. 1:18b-23.
      1) The hope of God's calling. 18b.
      2) The riches of the glory of His inheritance in the saints. 18c.
      3) The exceeding greatness of His power toward us. 1:19-23.
        a) This power used to raise Christ. 1:20a.
        b) This power used to exalt Christ. 1:20b-21.
        c) This power used to subject all things to Christ. 1:22a.
        d) This power used to make Christ head over the church. 1:22b-23.
          The church is His body. 1:23a.
          The church is His fulness. 1:23b.

In the foregoing section (1:3-14) we found a marvelous list of spiritual blessings that God has given us. But often Christians do not appreciate these spiritual blessings. Many church members actually appreciate material blessings (such as money) more than they do their spiritual blessings. But actually the spiritual blessings are greater than all others because they have the promise of both the life that now is, and that which is to come (I Tim. 5:8; II Cor. 4:18). No person who seeks first the kingdom of heaven will lack any necessary thing in this life. And only those who seek first the spiritual things have the promise of salvation in the life to come.

In this section we therefore find Paul praying that his readers might know and appreciate the spiritual blessings. Paul prayed every day for this. Many church members today are lukewarm, unconcerned, and unmindful of spiritual things. We should pray for such people, even as Paul did.

Fact Questions

71. What is the title of the section (1:15-23)?
72. Why are spiritual blessings greater than material blessings?
73. What three things did Paul pray that we would know?

Text (1:15, 16)

15 For this cause I also, having heard of the faith in the Lord Jesus which is among you, and the love which *ye show* toward all the saints, 16 cease not to give thanks for you, making mention *of you* in my prayers;

Thought Questions (1:15-16)

38. For what cause was it that Paul did not cease to pray for them?
39. Would you infer from the fact that Paul said he had *heard* of the faith of the Ephesians that (1) either Paul did not write the epistle, or (2) that it was not actually written to the Ephesians? Why or why not?
40. What was the attitude of the Ephesians toward all saints?
41. How regularly did Paul pray for the Ephesians?
42. Did Paul pray for them by name? Give a reason for your answer.

Paraphrase

15. For this reason, that ye were sealed with the Holy Spirit, and made recipients of many other blessings, I also, having heard of the commendable faith in the Lord Jesus which continues among you, and the love which you have toward all the saints, both Jew and Gentile,

16. do not cease to be giving thanks in behalf of you, making mention of you by name in my daily prayers.

Notes (1:15-16)

1. The *Interpreter's Bible* says about Ephesians 1:15 that these words belong to the literary fiction by which the epistle is represented as a message from Paul. Such conclusions are not supported by any evidence, only by personal opinion. The mere fact that Paul said that he had "heard" of the faith of the Ephesians, does not prove that he had never been with them. He wrote the same way to Philemon (4, 5), and similarly to the Thessalonians (I Thessalonians 3:6). Cer-

tainly Paul knew these people intimately. (See Introduction, sec. VIII for further information.)

2. Paul was glad to hear (perhaps from Tychicus) about the faith which the Ephesians had steadfastly held in the Lord Jesus, and their love for one another. The church at Ephesus was unusual in that it had both Jews and Gentiles in it, and they really loved one another. But Paul still prayed for them, thanking God for them, and asking God to further enlighten them.

Fact Questions

71. What two things had Paul heard about the Ephesians?

Text (1:17)

17 that the God of our Lord Jesus Christ, the Father of glory, may give unto you a spirit of wisdom and revelation in the knowledge of him;

Thought Questions (1:17)

43. What does the phrase, *the Father of glory,* mean?

44. Did Paul pray that God would reveal His truth directly to the Ephesians? Would not such a prayer contradict 3:3-4? What exactly did Paul want them to have that he calls *a spirit of wisdom and revelation?*

45. Why is a spirit of wisdom and revelation needed by the saints who have all already accepted Christ?

46. What is the significance of the spirit of wisdom and revelation being *in the knowledge of Him?* Who is the *Him?*

Paraphrase

17. Requesting that God, the glorious Father in heaven, who is adored as God even by our Lord Jesus Christ, and who originates both the glory we now enjoy and that greater glory we shall have hereafter, that He may give unto you a wise spirit and a spirit of revelation, that is, a disposition which will make you able and ready to receive that which He has revealed concerning the precise knowledge of Himself.

Notes (1:17)

1. See notes on 1:3 concerning the expression, *God of our Lord Jesus Christ.*

2. "The apostle did not pray that God would give to all the Ephesians the knowledge of the doctrines of the Gospel by an immediate revelation made to themselves. But that he would enable them to understand the revelation of these doctrines which was made to the apostles, and which they preached to the world." (Macknight)

3. The *spirit of wisdom and revelation* is described in 1:18 as *having the eyes of your heart enlightened*. How greatly Christians need to have a heart which is responsive to God and spiritual things: Many are like blind men standing in a lovely park in broad daylight. All around them lie riches of beauty, but they cannot see. There are treasures of wisdom and knowledge revealed in Christ (Col. 2:3). But many cannot see. They need to be taught the first principles over and over. Oh God, grant that throughout our churches a spirit may sweep which will cause our brethren to grasp the riches of Thy revelation:

4. God is not interested in anyone being wise and receptive to revelations unless they are revelations that are in the knowledge of God Himself. If He felt otherwise, He would have to deny Himself. (II Tim. 2:13)

Fact Questions

72. How does Paul describe God in 1:17?
73. What did Paul pray that God would give to the Ephesians?
74. In what must this spirit of wisdom and revelation rest?

Text (1:18, 19)

18 having the eyes of your heart enlightened, that ye may know what is the hope of his calling, what the riches of the glory of his inheritance in the saints, 19 and what the exceeding greatness of his power to us-ward who believe, according to that working of the strength of his might

Thought Questions (1:18-19)

47. What connection is there between the *spirit of wisdom and revelation* mentioned in v. 17, and the phrase *having the eyes of your heart enlightened* in v. 18?

48. So the heart has eyes! What is this heart that has *eyes?*
49. What is the *hope of his calling* that we are to know? Who is being called? By whom? How is the calling done? Doesn't every person who knows enough to accept Christ know the hope of His calling?
50. Who has an inheritance in the saints? What does He inherit? Why does this inheritance contain riches of glory?
51. What will be the benefit of knowing the exceeding greatness of God's power toward us?

Paraphrase

18. I pray that you may have a spirit of wisdom and revelation, so that the eyes of your heart (mind and understanding) may be enlightened with lasting illumination. Being thus enlightened, you may know what blessings are contained in the hope to which God has called you by the Gospel, and may know what are the riches of the glory of God's inheritance, which is His saints,

19. and that you may also know what is the exceeding greatness of the power which God employs toward us who believe, that power which is so great that it can be described only by saying that it is according to the working of the power of His strength.

Notes (1:18-19)

1. There is a great need for all of us to have the eyes of our hearts (understanding) enlightened. Many people are like Adam and Eve. They have had their eyes opened to sin by disobeying God. But it is usually much harder to have our eyes opened to good than to evil. We must learn fully about God's promises, glory, blessings, etc. Then we must live by what we know. Head knowledge without heart enlightenment is not good enough.

2. Paul lists three things we need to know through having the eyes of our heart enlightened:

    1) *The hope of His calling.* This refers to that living hope which we have in Christ of a heavenly inheritance that

46

fades not away (I Peter 1:3-4). God called us by the gospel, that good news about Christ which was preached to us (I Thess. 2:14). Some people accept Christ much as they buy fire insurance, as a matter of protection. Christ is truly your protection. Nonetheless we do not follow Christ just because we must, but because we cherish and seek after the *hope of His calling.*

2) *The riches of the glory of His* (God's) *inheritance in the saints.*

As stated in 1:11, the saints (Christians) are God's inheritance, His heritage. Naturally this brings great benefits to the saints, as well as pleasure to God. It is a rich and glorious arrangement. Christians can well apply Moses' words to themselves:

"The eternal God is thy dwelling place,

And underneath are the everlasting arms;

Happy art thou, O Israel (O church of God);

Who is like unto thee, a people saved by Jehovah?"

(Deut. 33:27, 29)

3) *The exceeding greatness of His power toward us that believe.*

God's people often act like they think that God cannot or will not do anything for them. We need the eyes of our heart enlightened to grasp the truth that the same power that God used for Jesus, He can and does put to work for us. This thought almost staggers the imagination. But it is true. Study the notes on 1:20-22 to see how God used His power in the life of Jesus, and remember that this is an illustration of the power he uses to deliver us from evil, rule providentially in our lives, and to raise us from the dead.

Fact Questions

75. According to 1:18, what needs to be enlightened?
76. What are the three things Paul prayed that we would know?
77. In what is God's inheritance?

EPHESIANS 1:18, 19

PAUL PRAYED THAT
WE WOULD KNOW ---

1. THE HOPE OF GOD'S CALLING.

2. THE RICHES OF THE GLORY OF HIS INHERITANCE IN THE SAINTS.

3. THE GREATNESS OF HIS POWER TOWARD US.

DO YOU KNOW THESE THINGS?

Text (1:20-23)

20 which he wrought in Christ, when he raised him from the dead, and made him to sit at his right hand in the heavenly *places*, 21 far above all rule, and authority, and power, and dominion, and every name that is named, not only in this world, but also in that which is to come; 22 and he put all things in subjection under his feet, and gave him to be head over all things to the church 23 which is his body, the fulness of him that filleth all in all.

Thought Questions (1:20-23)

52. What is that *which God wrought in Christ?* (See 1:19).
53. Why is the mighty power which God wrought in Christ described here?
54. If God's power raised Christ from the dead, what can it do for us?
55. Who will have the most honored name even in the world that is to come?
56. How can God have put all things in subjection under Christ's feet when the majority of humankind are in rebellion against Him? (Psalm 2 can help answer this question.)
57. Note that Christ is head over all things to the church. Name three areas of church affairs over which Christ is head.
58. What is the implication of the fact that the church is Christ's body? Does that suggest that the church exercises the authority of Christ? Or that the church is subject to Christ? Or that it is intimately joined to Christ?
59. To Whom does this refer "Him that filleth all in all" (1:23; cf. 4:10)?
60. What does the fact that the church is the *fulness* of Christ mean?

Paraphrase

20. (praying that you may know) that power which God put to work in the life of Christ, and will employ toward us that believe, when He raised Christ from the dead, and gave Him the honor of sitting at His own right hand in heaven as chief governor of the universe,

21. having seated Christ there by His power in spite of the efforts of wicked men, the devil, and death itself to destroy Christ. There Christ was seated far above all the ranks of authority held by men or spiritual creatures, whether they be first rulers, or authorities, or mighty powers, or lordships, yea above every name that is named, not only in this world, but even in that which is to come;

22. and further demonstrating His great power in the life of Christ, God did subject all things in the universe under his feet, and appointed Him supreme Lord and head over all things pertaining to the church,

23. which (the church) is His (Christ's) body and His fulness, that which is filled by Him who verily filleth all things in all places.

Notes (1:20-23)

1. Verses 20-23 are an elaboration of v. 19. Paul prayed that we would know what is the exceeding greatness of God's power toward us. This power is described as being the power that God used for Jesus. It is almost staggering to think that we have available unto us the same power that God used for Christ. But that is true. Note what God did for Jesus:

    1) He raised Him from the dead. 1:20. If we believe that God raised up Jesus from the dead, we ought to have strong confidence, for God will use this same great power by which He raised up Jesus to help us.

    2) God exalted Jesus by seating Him at His right hand in heaven (Mark 16:19; Psalm 110:1). God exalted Jesus far above all principality, power, might and dominion, and every name that is named, not only in this age, but in that which is to come. The "principalities, powers, might, and dominions" mentioned here seem to refer to ranks and degrees of power among angels and spiritual beings, both good and bad (Col. 1:16; Eph. 6:12).

    3) God put all things beneath the feet of Christ; He is Lord of all — heaven, earth, hades, hell, angels, governments, and all (Matthew 28:18).

4) God made Christ to be head over all things to the church, which is His body, the fulness of Him that filleth all things in all places.

The word *fulness* etymologically has a passive sense (Thayer), signifying *that which is filled*. This is a wonderful thought. The church is filled (not just allotted a sample) *by* Christ with blessings and salvation. The church is to be filled *for* Christ with holiness, service, and worship.

Note that there is only one head over the church, and that Christ is that head. He is head over *all things* to the church: its worship, its laws, its plan of salvation, its moral standards, etc. No pope, bishop, church council, convention, synod, prophet, preacher, or anyone else dares to rob Christ of any of the authority God gave to Him.

Note that the church is Christ's body. In the context here the principal suggestion is that Christ is the ruler (or head) over the church. He directs the church as a human head directs the body beneath it.

Christ has only one body, one church. Can you imagine a freak with one head, but a hundred bodies attached to the head? Surely such a monstrosity could not make any progress in any direction. Yet we must assume that such a monster exists today, if we assume that all the denominations are divine Christ has only one church. (See Eph. 4:4.)

2. There have been false applications made of the fact that the church is the body of Christ. It would be wrong to reason that since the church is the body of Christ, and is in a sense an extension of Christ Himself, that the church therefore exercises the authority of Christ on earth. This is the Roman Catholic position.

Ephesians 5:24 makes it very plain that the relationship of the body to the head is that of SUBJECTION. The church is subject to Christ the head in everything, and does not exercise authority for the head. The church cannot make laws for Christ. Neither can it accept nor reject any persons whom Christ has rejected or accepted.

3. Concerning the *heavenly places,* see note on 1:3.

4. We ought to pray, as Paul did, that we ourselves and all our brethren may have the eyes of our heart enlightened about these things.

Fact Questions

78. Name the four things God's power did for Christ.

79. Why are these demonstrations of God's power in the life of Christ mentioned?

80. What are the *rule, authority, power, and dominion* of v. 21?

81. What is the sense and meaning of the term *fulness?*

82. What is the body of Christ?

83. Who is the head of the church? Over what things in the church is He the head?

84. Why does the fact that the church is the fulness and body of Christ not give it the authority of Christ on earth?

EPHESIANS TWO

A DOUBLE-BARRELLED BLESSING
FOR GOD'S SAINTS

I. ONCE DEAD -- NOW ALIVE
   2:1-10

   1. Before Conversion -- Dead -- 2:1-3

   2. After Conversion -- Alive -- 2:4-10

II. ONCE ALIENS -- NOW FELLOW
    CITIZENS with the Saints -- 2:11-22

    1. Before Christ -- Aliens -- 2:12

    2. After Christ -- Made Nigh -- 2:13-18

    3. Grand Summary -- 2:19-22

Previewing in Outline Form (2:1-10)

C. Once dead, now alive with Christ. 2:1-10.

   1. Before conversion, dead through trespasses and sins. 2:1-3.

     a. Ye were sinful yourselves. 2:2.

       1) Walked according to the course of this world.

       2) Walked according to the Devil.

         a) The prince of the power of the air.

         b) The prince of the spirit that now works in the sons of disobedience.

     b. You associated with sinners. 2:3a.

       1) In the lusts of the flesh.

       2) Doing the desires of the flesh and mind.

     c. You were liable to suffer God's wrath because of sin. 2:3b.

   2. After conversion, made alive with Christ. 2:4-10.

     a. Made alive because God was rich in mercy. 2:4.

     b. Made alive though dead through trespasses. 2:5.

     c. Two blessings following being made alive. 2:6.

       1) Raised up with Jesus.

       2) Made to sit in heavenly places.

     d. Made alive that God might show the riches of His grace in the ages to come. 2:7.

     e. Made alive (saved) by grace through faith. 2:9-10.

       1) Not saved by ourselves.

       2) Saved by the gift of God.

       3) Not saved by our works. 2:9-10.

         a) We are God's workmanship. 2:10.

         b) However, we were created for good works. 2:10.

In this section we find the answer to the question, "How can living people be DEAD in sins?"

Strictly speaking, 2:1-10 is a continuation of Paul's description of God's great power toward us (1:19-23). Certainly God's power is demonstrated gloriously in the way He made us who were dead because of sins to be alive with Christ.

However, because the section is lengthy and is a well-defined paragraph in itself, it helps us to remember the contents of the chapter if we list this section as a separate topic in the outline. This we have done under the heading, "Once dead, now alive with Christ."

Fact Questions

85. What is the title of this section (2:1-10)?
86. What are its two main subdivisions and their Scripture limitations?

Text (2:1-3)

And you *did he make alive* when ye were dead through your trespasses and sins, 2 wherein ye once walked according to the course of this world, according to the prince of the powers of the air, of the spirit that now worketh in the sons of disobedience; 3 among whom we also all once lived in the lusts of our flesh, doing the desires of the flesh and of the mind, and were by nature children of wrath, even as the rest

Thought Questions (2:1-3)

61. What does *quickened* (King James Version, v. 1) mean?
62. Are we *dead* because of some original sin we inherited from Adam, or through some other means? (Read v. 1 carefully for the answer.)
63. Do those who are dead in sins have to be inactive, like those in the grave? Are the dead necessarily unconscious, asleep, or annihilated (Luke 9:60; Rev. 6:9-10)?
64. At what occasion were we made alive after being dead in trespasses and sins (Col. 2:12-13)?
65. Can you make any distinction between *trespasses* and *sins?* Try.
66. What is the character of the *course of this world?*
67. Who is the prince of the power of the air? Why is he called that? (See Rev. 12:9, 12; Eph. 6:12)
68. The word *prince* has two prepositional phrases that follow it. What is the second one?
69. What are *sons of disobedience?* What kind of a spirit works in them?
70. What are *children of wrath?* Whose wrath is referred to? What relationship do the children have to wrath?
71. What does it mean that we were *by nature* children of wrath? Is this some nature that we have inherited from Adam? Or is this some nature that we have cultivated ourselves?

Paraphrase

1. Even as God's great power did raise up Christ (1:20), He did also make you Ephesians alive when you were dead (cut

55

off from God) because of your trespasses and sins.

2. Before your conversion you did walk in these trespasses and sins, according to the present sinful age of the world, according to the Devil, the ruler of the power of evil which has its residence in the air, and also the ruler (or author) of that rebellious spirit which now works in those who disobey God.

3. Among these children of disobedience we all, Jews and Gentiles, at one time lived our lives, interested only in the desires of the flesh, following the inclinations of the flesh and of our corrupt minds, until evil had become part of our nature, and we had become, without ever realizing it, children doomed to suffer God's wrath, just like the rest of humankind.

Notes

1. The words in v. 1 that are in italics are, of course, not in the original Greek text. They are supplied from 2:5 to make the sense more apparent, and are a helpful addition at this place. *Quickened* in the King James Version means *made alive.*

2. The person who is a sinner is *dead* as far as God is concerned. In the Bible death does NOT imply unconsciousness, or annihilation, or going out of existence. Both the good and evil are still conscious after physical death (Rev. 6:9-10; Luke 16:22-24; Isa. 14:9-10). Death is simply a *complete change of relationships,* or a *separation* from former relationships. When people are alive here on earth, we can talk to them and deal with them. When they die, the relationships are changed. We can no longer talk with them and deal with them. But they can then see and be with others who have died, and with the angels and the Lord Jesus (if they are saved).

   Now when a person is dead in sins, he can still walk around among us. But he is as cut off from God as a man in the grave is cut off from us. God cannot bless such a *dead* person, or answer his prayers, or take him to heaven. It was in this way that Adam and Eve died on the very day they ate the forbidden fruit (Gen. 2:17). (Of course, they obviously received pardon afterwards through the offering of sacrifices in anticipation of the death of Christ.)

   There is hope, however, even for those who are dead in sins. Jesus said, "The hour is coming and NOW IS, when the dead (spiritually) shall hear the voice of the Son of God; and they that hear shall live (John 5:25; cf. Jn. 2:28-29). When we hear the gospel, believe in Christ, repent, and are baptized, our relationships change again. We are no longer dead IN sins, but we are dead TO sin and alive unto God (Romans 6:11).

3. *Trespass* may refer to a willful sin. *Sin* means *missing the true mark of life,* and is a general term for sin.

4. The Greek text does not say that we are dead *in* trespasses and sins, but *because of* or *by* or *through* trespasses and sins.

5. Note that sinners walk according to two things:
   1) According to the course of this world.
   2) According to the prince of the power of the air (Satan), who is also the prince (or author) of the wicked disposition that now works in those who disobey God.

   Most sinners would deny emphatically that they are directed by any outside influence. They pride themselves on being so emancipated that they can do what they please, not realizing that this is Satan's method of directing their lives, and that Satan is the prince of the spirit that directs their life.

6. *Prince of the power of the air.* Satan apparently dwells in the air (and WHERE do we not contact the air?). He has his angels organized into an efficient power.

   Paul plainly teaches the existence of a real devil in these verses, and we believe it. Some modern interpreters deny that there is a real Devil. For example, it is stated in the *Interpreter's Bible* that the idea of a personal Devil is all but unimaginable to the mind of our times, and is capable of interpretation only as a personification of the external forces of evil which play upon human life. Such adiabolism must amuse his majesty, Prince Satan. He is not the least offended when people deny his existence. In fact, it is most gratifying to him.

7. We who are now Christians all once lived as disobedient children, just like the people who live around us. *Conversation* (King James Version, v. 3) means *manner of life.* We did whatever the lusts (or desires) of our flesh craved and whatever our minds (often lazy, filthy, and scheming) thought of. We were by nature *children of wrath,* even as the rest of humankind. We were not relatives of wrath, but the

very children against whom God's wrath was directed because of our sins.

8. The fact that we were *by nature* children of wrath does not imply that we were born into the world with God's wrath upon us because of some guilt we inherited from Adam. *Nature* here refers to conduct practiced so long and habitually that it has become our natural way of living. The apostle speaks of men being by nature children of wrath as the effect (rather than the cause) of our trespasses and sins. The quibble advanced by some theologians that, "We are not sinners because we sin; we sin because we are sinners," lays all the blame for our sins upon Adam (or upon GOD) instead of upon ourselves where it belongs. Numerous passages teach that children are *not born condemned* and subject to God's wrath (Matt. 19:14; Rom. 5:18; etc.).

Fact Questions

87. From what verse are the words *did He make alive* supplied into v. 1?
88. What is the condition of the sinner as far as God is concerned (2:1)?
89. How is death defined in the notes?
90. Explain how living people can be dead in sins.
91. According to what two things did we walk before our conversion (v. 2)?
92. What does the word *conversation* (used in the King James Version, 2:3) mean?
93. The desires of what two things are done by the children of disobedience?
94. Now that you have studied the lesson, go back and review the thought questions.

Text (2:4, 5)

4 but God, being rich in mercy for his great love wherewith he loved us, 5 even when we were dead through our trespasses, made us alive together with Christ (by grace have ye been saved)

Thought Questions (2:4, 5)

72. Is there reason for which we deserve to be treated with mercy by God?
73. What was it that made God be merciful to us?

74. With Whom were we made alive? What kind of a resurrection was this? Does 2:5 imply that Christ was spiritually
dead?

Paraphrase

4. But though we were children who deserved to suffer God's
wrath, God was rich in mercy toward us on account of the
surpassing love He had toward us.
5. Therefore, even though we were dead (cut off from Him)
through our trespasses, He did make us alive together with
Christ. Thus it was by grace we were saved with a lasting
salvation. It is a favor which we do not deserve.

Notes

1. Oh the soul-thrilling meaning in that word, *but*: Because we
have all at one time walked according to the Devil, it would
be natural for the next verse to say, "AND God smote you
in His wrath." But such is not the case, praise God!
2. God was merciful to us because of the love He had for us.
The expression, *love wherewith He loved us*, is a Hebrew
way of describing the greatness of His love. We marvel that
it could be that God was not just merciful to us, but
LOVING.
3. Only through an out-and-out favor from God have we
been saved. The word *saved* is in the perfect tense, which
indicates a past action with continued efforts.
4. The fact that we have been made alive with Christ (Col.
2:13) does not indicate that Christ was spiritually dead. He
was, and is, alive; we have been made alive with Him.

Fact Questions

95. Why did God make us alive with Christ?
96. By what have we been saved?

Text (2:6, 7)

6 and raised us up with him, and made us to sit with him in the
heavenly *places* in Christ Jesus: 7 that in the ages to come he
might show the exceeding riches of his grace in kindness toward
us in Christ Jesus:

Thought Questions (2:6-7)

75. What similarities are there between what God did for Christ
(1:20), and what God has done for us (2:5-6)?

76. What are the *heavenly places* in which we sit? (See the notes on 1:3.)

77. How long will praise be offered to God for His grace toward us? (Compare Revelation 7:9-12; 15:3-4.)

78. In (or by) what does God demonstrate the exceeding riches of His grace?

Paraphrase

6. And God has raised us up from the state of death in which we existed before our conversion, and has made us alive together with Christ, and has made us to sit with Him in the heavenly places that are in Christ Jesus, that is, in the Christian church.

7. God has done this so that He might show throughout the ages which are to come the exceeding riches of His favor toward us by the kindness which He has extended unto us in Christ Jesus in making us spiritually alive and giving us a glorious and heavenly standing in the church.

Notes (2:6-7)

1. Not only did God make us alive together with Christ, but He has also (1) raised us up spiritually with Christ, and (2) made us to sit with Christ in the heavenly places, the church. The *heavenly places* mentioned here cannot refer to heaven for we do not sit bodily in heaven as Jesus does (1:20). But are members of the church of Christ, which is a heavenly institution.

2. God desires the praise due unto His name. God has favored us very greatly because of His love. But He has also favored us because He desires the sincere praise of loving souls. In all the ages to come, even after Jesus returns, we shall be praising God's riches of grace which He has demonstrated by kindness toward us in Christ Jesus.

Fact Questions

97. Besides making us alive, what two things has God done for us?

98. What does God wish to show forth in ages to come?

Text (2:8-10)

8 for by grace have ye been saved through faith; and that not of yourselves, *it is* the gift of God; 9 not of works, that no man

should glory. 10 For we are his workmanship, created in Christ
Jesus for good works, which God afore prepared that we should
walk in them.

Thought Questions (2:8-10)

79. If salvation by grace through faith is not of ourselves, from
Whom does it come?
80. What is it that is the *gift of god*? Grace? Salvation? Faith?
Is faith a gift of God (Rom. 10:17)?
81. Is the doctrine of salvation by works held by many people in
these times? Why would being saved by works give a person
an opportunity to glory (boast)?
82. Whose workmanship has made the converted man what he is?
83. For what purpose were we *created in Christ Jesus*?
84. What is it that God afore prepared that we should walk in?
What preparation did He make that we should do this?
When did He make this preparation?
85. If good works are so essential after conversion, why are
they disconnected from conversion?

Paraphrase

8. For (as I said in v. 5) you have been saved purely by the
favor (grace) of God through faith. This salvation is no
work of yours; it is the free gift of God who might have
suffered the human race to perish. Thus our salvation will
always be something that will bring forth praise to God.
(2.:7)
9. Salvation, being the gift of God, is not obtained by doing
good works before our conversion. No man will have opportunity to boast that he has earned his salvation by works.
10. For we are what we are as Christians as a result of God's
workmanship. And yet, while our salvation is not earned by
good deeds which we did, we were created by God (at our
conversion) for this very purpose, to do good works. God
made preparation when He sent Christ into the world that
we should become a transformed people who would give
constant attention to doing good.

Notes

1. Paul here repeats and enlarges upon a thought already given
by him in the letter, namely that we have been saved by
grace through faith (2:5; 1:6). In the New Testament *faith*

implies not only belief, but obedience as well (Gal. 2:26-27). "You are all the children of God by *faith* in Christ Jesus. *For as many of you as have been baptized into Christ have put on Christ.*"

2. The expression, *that not of yourselves, it is the gift of God,* refers neither to grace nor faith. *That* which is not of ourselves refers to the whole affair of being saved by grace through faith. This salvation by grace through faith is all the gift of God. Our works had nothing to do with it. We cannot boast about how good we are. We were not saved because of any goodness we have, even though God expects us to do good. Even a man as good as Cornelius was not saved by his goodness (Acts 10:1-3; 11:13-14). Actually, all our goodness does not impress God as beautiful adornment for our souls; it is like filthy rags (Isa. 64:6).

3. We are God's workmanship, that which God has made. No Christian should feel that he is self-made. Without God's plan of salvation through Christ, even the best of us would be utterly lost.

Nonetheless, we were created by God through Christ Jesus for good works. This *creation* refers to our spiritual creation, which took place at conversion (II Cor. 5:17). If we do not do good works, we defeat God's purpose in giving us His favor. God made many preparations (such as sending Christ, the Holy Spirit, etc.) that all whom He would save should live doing good works.

4. As we come to the close of this section, entitled "Once dead, now alive with Christ," we think of the people who have told us (at great length sometimes) how they recovered from some deadly sickness in the hospital. The Christian can glory, not just that he has recovered from a great illness, but that HE VERILY HAS BEEN MADE ALIVE FROM THE DEAD!

Fact Questions

99. By what and through what have we been saved?
100. In the New Testament what does *faith* imply besides belief?
101. What is it that is the *gift of God*?
102. By what is our salvation NOT obtained?
103. In what did God prepare that we should walk?

Previewing in Outline Form (2:11-22)

D. Once aliens, now fellow-citizens with the saints. 2:11-22.
(This section is addressed to Gentile Christians. 2:11.)

1. Former condition — far off. 2:12.
   a. Separate from Christ.
   b. Alienated from the commonwealth of Israel.
      (An alien is a foreign-born resident of a country, in which he does not possess the privileges of a citizen.)
   c. Strangers from the covenants of the promise.
   d. Having no hope.
   e. Without God in the world.

2. Present condition — made nigh in Christ's blood. 2:13-18.
   a. He (Christ) is our peace. 2:14.
   b. He makes both Jews and Gentiles one. 2:14-18.

   1) He broke down the middle wall of partition between them, abolishing in His flesh the law of commandments. 2:14b-16.
      a) He did this that He might create in Himself one new man of the two. 2:15b.
      b) He did this to reconcile both unto God in one body. 2:16.
   2) He preached peace to those far off and those that were nigh. 2:17.
      a) He provides access to the Father for both Jews and Gentiles. 2:18.

3. Grand summary. 2:19-22.
   a. We are no more strangers and sojourners. 2:19.
   b. We are fellow-citizens with the saints.
   c. We are members of the household of God.
   d. We are built upon the foundation of the apostles and prophets, Christ being the chief corner-stone. 2:20-22.
      1) In Him all the building grows into a holy temple. 2:21.
      2) In Him ye are builded together for an habitation of God. 2:22.

Fact Questions

104. What is the section 2:11-22 called?
105. What are the subdivisions of this section?
106. What is an alien?

Text (2:11-12)

11 Wherefore remember, that once ye, the Gentiles in the flesh, who are called Uncircumcision by that whic his called Circumcision, in the flesh, made by hands; 12 that ye were at that time separate from Christ, alienated from the commonwealth of Israel, and strangers from the covenants of the promise, having no hope and without God in the world.

Thought Questions (2:11-12)

86. What is the benefit of remembering the bad character of our ancestors who lived before Christ came to earth?

87. What was the feeling held by the Jew toward those he called *Uncircumcision*?

88. How would the Gentiles be any more separate from Christ (the Messiah) than the Jews were before Christ came?

89. What misfortune was it to the Gentiles to be *alienated from the commonwealth of Israel*?

90. What is a *covenant*? How many promises were attached to the covenants referred to? What was the promise? Name any individuals with whom God made a covenant containing the promise.

91. Are there still people who have no hope and are without God in the world? Is such a conditon any longer necessary?

Paraphrase

11. Wherefore, to strengthen your sense of God's goodness in saving you (2:8), and of the obligation that He has thereby laid on you to do good works (2:10), you Ephesians should remember that you were formerly Gentiles by natural descent, people who are called "Uncircumcised" and "Unholy" by the nation (the Jews) which is called "Circumcised" with a circumcision made with men's hands on the flesh, and which considers itself holy on that account and entitled to the promises.

12. Remember always that you were at that time before Christ came, without any knowledge or hope of the Messiah, which the Jews knew and rejoiced in; you were alienated from the state of Israel, which God had chosen as His own people (Deut. 14:2); you were unacquainted with the covenants (agreements and arrangements) such as God made with Abraham and David that contained the promise of the

Messiah; having no hope of immortality or forgiveness of sins; and without God and the life that He imparts (4:18).

Notes (2:11-12)

1. Remembering the darkness in which our ancestors lived before Christ came (and in which we would still be living if He had not come) should make us humble and devoted to good works in the name of Christ.

2. We often boast of our superior American civilization, and sometimes even of our "superior" white race. We need to remember that before Christ came our ancestors practiced human sacrifice in Britian (among the Druids). The savagery of the Irish, the Gauls (French), and the Germans was no better. All the good within us and within our society has come to us through the Christ. But many snub (and indeed crucify) the Christ who has so abundantly favored us.

3. "There are those delightful English (and American) people so broadminded that they would let the heathen alone (and not send missionaries to them). Where did these delightful large-minded Christians come from? From heathendom. There was a time when their ancestors painted themselves blue, and did not wear any clothing worth mentioning, and were not indisposed to eat one another when circumstances seemed to point in the direction of that kind of gruesome festival. Yet these people who have come from heathenism gather their fur cloaks around them and say that perhaps it would be just as well to let the heathen alone. Persons who talk so never saw Christ, never felt the power of His love, have absolutely nothing whatever to do with Christ; and when they touch the cup of His blood, they bring their blasphemy to a culmination." (Joseph Parker)

4. The hopelessness of the Gentiles before Christ came is well illustrated by an ancient letter from one woman to another. The writer of the letter had previously lost a son, and was writing to console another woman who had lost her son some time later:

"Irene to Taonnophris and Philo, good comfort. I am so sorry and weep over the departed one as I wept for Didymas. And all things, whatsoever were fitting, I have done, and all mine, Epaphroditus, and Thurmuthian, and Philion, and Appollonius and Plantas. But nevertheless, against such things one can do nothing.

Therefore comfort ye one another. Farewell." (From Rimmer, *Crying Stones*. Used by permission.)

5. God made numerous covenants with individuals (and groups) in Old Testament times that contained the promise of the Messiah (Christ). Examples are 1) the covenant with Abraham (Gen. 22:15-18; Gal. 3:15-16); 2) with David (II Sam. 7:12-16); 3) with Joshua, the high priest (Zechariah 3:6-8); 4) with all who hunger and thirst (Isaiah 55:3-5).

But the Gentiles knew nothing of these gracious, glowing *covenants of the promise*. They were strangers to them.

Fact Questions

107. Name four of the five things stated that the Gentiles did not have before Christ.
108. What promise did the *covenants of the promise* contain?

Text (2:13)

13 But now in Christ Jesus ye that once were far off are made nigh in the blood of Christ.

Thought Questions (2:13)

92. Who are those who were far off? Far off from what (2:12)?
93. In Whom are those who were once far off now made nigh?
94. Why is the blood of Christ needed to make us nigh?

Paraphrase

13. But now, in contrast to your former far-off and hopeless state, you Gentiles who are in Christ Jesus, that is, in His body, the church, are made to be near to God through the blood that Jesus shed to bring us unto God. (I Peter 3:18)

Notes (2:13)

1. What a contrast is indicated by that little word *but*. It implies all the difference between the savagery of heathenism, and godly civilized people who call on the name of the Lord.

2. No man can hope to be brought near to God except by the precious blood of Christ.

Fact Questions

109. In what are the Gentiles made nigh?

Text (2:14-16)

14 **For he is our peace, who made both one, and brake down the middle wall of partition, 15 having abolished in his flesh the enmity,** *even* **the law of commandments** *contained* **in ordinances; that he might create in himself of the two one new man,** *so* **making peace; 16 and might reconcile them both in one body unto God through the cross, having slain the enmity thereby:**

Thought Questions (2:14-16)

95. Who is our peace? What does it mean when it says, *He is our peace?*

96. Who are the *both* that were made one?

97. What was the middle wall of partition between Jews and Gentiles? Verse 15 can give you the answer to this.

98. How did the Law of commandments cause enmity between Jew and Gentile?

99. When did Christ abolish the Law of Commandments? (See Col. 2:14.)

100. Can you see the appropriateness in the description of the united Jews and Gentiles as *one new MAN?* (See 1:23)

101. In Whom did Christ create the Jews and Gentiles into *one new man?*

102. Note that both Jews and Gentiles need to be reconciled unto someone. Unto Whom (v. 16)

103. In what one body were both Jews and Gentiles reconciled?

104. If the *enmity* of v. 15 is the enmity between Jew and Gentile, between whom is the *enmity* of v. 16?

Paraphrase

14. For Christ is the author of the peace that we have with one another and with God. He has made both Jew and Gentile to be one people of God, and He has abolished the law of Moses which served as a partition between Jews and Gentiles for centuries.

15. He broke down this middle wall of partition when He died upon the cross, and thereby abolished the law of Moses with its commandments in the form of ordinances, such as circumcision, meats, washings, and holy days, that He might create the two (Jew and Gentile) into one new man in His own body (the church), thus making peace between them.

16. Christ abolished the law of commandments that He might reconcile completely both Jew and Gentile into one body (church), reconciling them unto God through the cross,

having by it (the cross) slain the sinful passions of both Jews and Gentiles, which were the cause of their enmity toward God.

Notes (2:14-16)

1. An illustration of the barrier, *the middle wall of partition,* between Jews and Gentiles before the Christian age can be seen in the signs placed at the gates leading into the inner courts of the temple in Jerusalem, warning the Gentiles not to go farther. One sign read, "No foreigner is allowed within that balustrade and embankment about the sanctuary. Whoever is caught (violating this rule) will be personally responsible for his ensuing death."

2. The enmity between Jews and Gentiles is well demonstrated by Peter's statement to Cornelius: "Ye know how that it is an unlawful thing for a man that is a Jew to keep company, or come unto one of another nation" (Acts 10:28). Note also that the Jews would not come into the house of Pilate (John 18:28-29).

3. The ceremonies of the Law made (and still make) the Jews peculiar in the eyes of the Gentiles. Consider their peculiar diet and Sabbath laws for example. "Their laws are diverse from all the people; neither keep they the king's laws" (Esther 3:8).

   But the Law also caused the Jews to look down on the Gentiles. To them anyone who did not keep the law was almost beneath contempt.

   At one time the Law served the very needful purpose of keeping the Jews separated from the idolatry of the Gentiles. But after the Savior of the whole world came, there was no need to keep them separated longer.

4. Few of us would be Christians today if we had to keep all the customs of Moses, to say nothing of all the traditions of the Jewish rabbis. We thank God, then, that when Christ came and died, He abolished in His flesh the commandments contained in the form of ordinances (Col. 1:20-22). When this barrier between the Jews and Gentiles was removed, the Gentiles could join the Jews in one body.

5. Christ abolished the Law for two reasons:
   1) To create the Jews and Gentiles into one body (church).
   2) To reconcile both unto God 2:16.

6. The *enmity* of v. 15 refers to the enmity between Jew and

Gentile. The *enmity* in v. 16 probably refers to the enmity between all men and God. It is a universal rule that whenever anyone does a harm or injustice to another, that the person who has done wrong will hold enmity against the one he has wronged, even if the one who is wronged forgives him. When any man is a sinner, he has enmity against God because of his evil works (Col. 1:21).

However, there is no stronger persuasion to move the sinner to be reconciled to God than that furnished by the death of Christ.

Fact Questions

110. What did Christ break down?
111. What was the cause of the enmity between Jews and Gentiles?
112. Into what did Christ create the two (Jews and Gentiles)?
113. What two purposes did Christ have in mind when He abolished the Law?
114. What did Christ slay through the cross? (v. 16)

Text (2:17, 18)

17 and he came and preached peace to you that were far off, and peace to them that were nigh: 18 for through him we both have our access in one Spirit unto the Father.

Thought Questions (2:17-18)

105. Who was it that *came and preached*?
106. Had Christ preached to the Ephesians personally (Matt. 15:24)? If not, how can it be said that *He preached peace to you*?
107. Who are those far off, and those who are nigh?
108. What is an *access*?
109. What is the one Spirit? How does the Spirit give us access to the Father?

Paraphrase

17. And Christ, having come in the person of His apostles and preachers, preached good tidings of peace to you Gentiles who were far off from God and to the Jews who were near to God because of their privileged position in ages past.
18. Thus Christ accomplished His work of making the Jews and Gentiles one, because that through Him, we both (Jews and

Gentiles) have the way of approach and the introduction unto the Father by the one Spirit that was given to both of us.

Notes (2:17-18)

1. After Christ had removed the Law as a barrier between Jew and Gentile by dying on the cross, He came (not personally, but through His Apostles and preachers, John 13:20), and preached good tidings of peace to the Gentiles who were far off (v. 13), and to the Jews who were near. As a rule, the Jews were closer to God than the Gentiles, for they had known the true God for centuries, while God had allowed the Gentiles to walk in their own ways.

2. Through Christ both the Jews and Gentiles have the access (way of approach and introduction) to the Father (God) by the one Holy Spirit. No one can talk to a king unless he is introduced by the proper people. Through Christ we can come into the Father's presence, whether we be Jew or Gentile, for Christ has given to us both the same Holy Spirit. And the Holy Spirit makes intercession for us. (See Romans 8:26)

Fact Questions

115. What did Christ preach?
116. To what two classes of people did Christ come and preach?
117. How can Christ be said to have preached to the Ephesians?
118. What do we have unto the Father through Christ?
119. In what do we have our access unto the Father?

Text (2:19, 20)

19 So then ye are no more strangers and sojourners, but ye are fellow-citizens with the saints, and of the household of God, 20 being built upon the foundation of the apostles and prophets, Christ Jesus himself being the chief corner stone;

Thought Questions (2:19-20)

110. What is the cause that we are no longer strangers and sojourners (2:17-18)? What do the words *strangers* and *sojourners* mean?

111. Who are the *saints* with whom we are now fellow-citizens?

112. What is the *household of God*?

70

113. According to I Corinthians 3:11, Christ is the only found-dation. How, then, can we be built upon the foundation of the apostles and prophets?

114. Are the prophets referred to here the Old Testament prophets or the New Testament prophets? What reasons do you give for your answer?

115. What would be the purposes of a chief corner-stone?

Paraphrase

19. Therefore then, seeing that you Gentiles have equal access to the Father in the one church with the Jews, you are no longer strangers to the covenants of the promise, nor out-siders dwelling by the people of God (2:12), but you are joint-citizens with the saints (the Israelites), and are members of the household of God, the church, which constitutes His temple (I Cor. 3:16; Heb. 3:6).

20. Being built into the church with the Jews upon the founda-tion laid by the apostles and prophets, namely upon Christ Jesus Himself, Who is the stone at the extreme corner, uniting the walls into one building.

Notes (2:19-20)

1. As a result of what Christ has done in abolishing the law of Moses and making peace between Jew and Gentile and be-tween all men and God, we (Gentile Christians) are no longer strangers (foreigners, aliens) and outsiders, but we are fellow-citizens with the saints, the Jewish Christians, and we all belong to the household (or family) of God, which is the church.

2. We have heard immigrants to the United States tell of their happy experiences in our free country. If it is wonderful to be a citizen in the U.S.A., it is MARVELOUS to be a citizen of the kingdom of God.

3. The foundation of the apostles and prophets is the foundation laid by the apostles and prophets in preaching Christ. "For other foundation can no man lay than that which is laid, which is *Jesus Christ*" (I Cor. 3:11).

4. The prophets mentioned here are probably those prophets who lived in the times of the apostles, the New Testament prophets such as Agabus, Silas, etc. (Acts 11:27-28; 13:1; 15:32; Eph. 3:5). Our reasons for believing this are as follows:

71

1) The prophets are listed after the apostles. Certainly the Old Testament prophets came before the apostles in time, but the New Testament prophets followed the apostles.

2) The Old Testament prophets taught the people to observe the law of Moses (Malachi 4:4). How could they be the foundation of the church, when the Law was the wall of partition between the Jew and Gentile (2:14-15)?

3) The Old Testament prophets desired to know the gospel of Christ, but were never permitted to know it (I Pet. 1:10-12). They could hardly, then, be the foundation of Christ's church.

4) The New Testament prophets would be more familiar to the predominantly Gentile church in Ephesus than the Old Testament prophets.

5) The reference to the *apostles and prophets* in 3:5 certainly has reference to the New Testament prophets.

5. In the temple of God, Christ Jesus is the chief corner stone. This stone was larger than the other stones, and was placed at the extreme corner where the two walls met. It thus united the two walls into one building, and gave strength to the whole building. The two walls are the Gentiles and Jews, united by Christ into one church.

6. What a precious privilege this is to know that we are builded upon Christ Jesus into the temple of God. We are built upon a better foundation than the temple of Diana, which sat only upon wooden piles driven deeply into the earth.

7. To the Christians at Ephesus, dwelling in the shadow of the great temple of Diana and daily seeing its outward grandeur, the references in this epistle to that spiritual building of which Christ was the cornerstone, and they a part of its noble superstructure, must have spoken with a force, an appropriateness, and a reassuring depth of meaning that cannot be overestimated.

Fact Questions

120. If we are no longer strangers and foreigners from God, what are we (2:19)?

121. What is the *foundation of the apostles and prophets*?

122. Who is the *chief cornerstone*? What is a chief cornerstone like, and what does it do?

123. What are the walls which are united by the chief corner-stone?

124. Why would the reference to the temple of God be especially appropriate to the Ephesians?

Text (2:21, 22)

21 in whom each several building, fitly framed together, groweth into a holy temple in the Lord; 22 in whom ye also are builded together for a habitation of God in the Spirit.

Thought Questions (2:21-22)

116. Who is referred to by the *Whom* of v. 21?
117. What is *each several building*? Does this refer to individuals, the church as a whole, denominations, or congregations?
118. How is each several building prepared so as to grow (v. 21)?
119. Into what does *each several building* grow?
120. Can we build the temple of God with hands? Why or why not?
121. How does God inhabit His temple?
122. Does God's Spirit dwell in His temple as a whole, or in the individual souls in it?

Paraphrase

21. In Christ, the chief cornerstone, the building, the universal church, being joined together in a harmonious way, is growing by the addition of converts into a holy temple (or sanctuary) in the Lord.

22. In which temple (or, in Whom) you (both Jews and Gentiles) are being builded together for a habitation of God, Who inhabits it not in any visible symbol, such as the statue of Diana, or even the glory in the tabernacle, but by the Holy Spirit, Who dwells in you both as individuals and as a body (I Cor. 3:16; 6:16).

Notes (2:21-22)

1. We interpret the phrase *each several building* as referring to the universal church, as the King James Version says, "all the building," or "the whole building." This harmonizes with the context which refers to Christ as the chief cornerstone of all the church.

73

The word *building* refers to an individual congregation in I Cor. 3:9. And here in Eph. 2:22 individuals are spoken of as being *builded* together. But we still prefer the interpretation we have given.

Certainly *each several building* does not refer to various denominations which all together make up the universal church. You cannot make a scriptural unit by combining many unscriptural units.

2. In Christ all the building (or *each several building*) *is fitly framed together*. (This same expression is used in 4:16 to describe the church as the body of Christ.) Truly the enmity between Jews and Gentiles, and the enmity between all men and God is broken down in the church, and thus every part is *fitly framed together* into one structure. It is necessary for it to be *fitly framed together* before it will grow.

3. In the tabernacle in the wilderness and the temple of Solomon, God dwelt in the cloud of glory. But now God dwells in the spiritual temple (the church) through the Holy Spirit in the individual believers. Also the Spirit dwells in them as congregations I Cor. 3:16.

4. Not only does the whole church grow into a holy temple in the Lord, but each individual believer is personally builded into the habitation for God in the Spirit. Being a part of church fellowship at its greatest extent is necessary. But unless each individual is a perfectly formed building stone, there will never be any great temple formed of many stones. We have to have both an individual relationship to Christ, and then also full participation with other saints in the church. Are you a living stone in the temple of God (I Pet. 2:14)?

Fact Questions

125. What phrase of three words describes the condition of the building that grows?
126. Into what does all the building grow?
127. For what are we builded together?
128. How does God inhabit His spiritual temple?

EPHESIANS THREE

PAUL'S PRAYER FOR

OUR STRENGTHENING

1. **BEGINNING OF PRAYER; 3:1**

2. **PARENTHETICAL -- PAUL'S MINISTRY OF THE MYSTERY OF CHRIST -- 2-13**

   a. Can Be Known By Reading -- 4

   c. Revealed That The Gentiles Are Fellow-Heirs -- 6

   d. Preaching The Mystery Makes Known God's Wisdom Through The Church -- 10

3. **PRAYER COMPLETED; 3:14-19**

   a. That We Be Strengthened Through God's Spirit -- 16

   b. That Christ Dwell In Our Hearts -- 17

   c. The We Comprehend B,L,H,&D -- 18

   d. That We Be Filled Unto All The Fulness Of God -- 19

   GLORIOUS DOXOLOGY; 3:20-21

Previewing in Outline Form (3:1-19)

E. Paul's prayer for our strengthening. 3:1-19.

  1. Beginning of prayer. 3:1.

  2. Parenthetical — Paul's ministry of the mystery of Christ. 3:2-13.

    a. The mystery was made known by revelation. 3:2-3.

    b. The mystery can be known by reading Paul's writings. 3:4.

    c. The mystery was unknown in previous ages. 3:5.

    d. The mystery concerns the Gentiles' equal privileges. 3:6.

    e. Paul, though undeserving, was appointed to preach the mystery. 3:7-9.

    f. Preaching the mystery is intended to make known the wisdom of God by the church. 3:10-12.

      (1) The mystery is to be made known to the principalities and powers. 3:10.

      (2) Made known according to God's eternal purpose in Christ. 3:11.

        (a) In Christ we have boldness and access. 3:12.

    g. Paul's request that they faint not at his sufferings. 3:13.

  3. The prayer completed. 3:14-19.

    a. Offered on bended knees to the Father. 3:14-15.

    b. Petitions.* 3:16-19.

*In the Greek text, three of these petitions are introduced by *hina.* The first *hina* clause has a compound object, which includes petitions (1) and (2) in our outline.

      (1) That you may be strengthened through God's Spirit in the inner man. 3:16.

      (2) That Christ may dwell in your hearts. 3:17.

      (3) That you may be able to comprehend the breadth, length, height, and depth. 3:17b-19a.

        (a) Made possible by being rooted and grounded in love. 3:17b.

        (b) Includes knowing the love of Christ that passes knowledge. 3:19.

      (4) That you may be filled unto all the fulness of God. 3:19b.

Fact Questions

129. What is section 3:1-19 called in the outline?

130. What is the parenthetical section about? What are the Scripture limitations of it?
131. What are the four petitions which Paul asked for the Ephesians?

Text (3:1)

For this cause I Paul, the prisoner of Christ Jesus, in behalf of you Gentiles

Thought Questions (3:1)

123. What was the cause referred to in the phrase, "for this cause"? Reread the preceding paragraph to find out.
124. Of whom was Paul a prisoner, Christ or Rome? Explain.
125. How did Paul's imprisonment help us Gentiles?

Paraphrase

1. Because of the glorious mystery which I know and preach, namely that the Gentiles are equal in privileges with the Jews, and are united in one church with them (2:16), and are not obligated to keep the law of Moses, I Paul, the prisoner (not of Rome, but of Christ Jesus), why by my imprisonment performs a protective ministry over you Gentiles — I do bow my knees unto the Father in prayer for you. (3:14)

Notes (3:1)

1. Paul was a bound prisoner, one bearing a chain. Ephesians 6:20.
2. Paul was technically the prisoner of the Jews and Romans, but he was in truth only the prisoner of Christ Jesus. If his heart had not been bound by chains of love, gratitude, duty, trust, and faith in Christ Jesus, he would soon have been free of his iron chains. But even when free of chains, he was always the prisoner of Christ and His service.
3. Paul was truly THE prisoner of Christ Jesus in behalf of us Gentiles. Others had been in prison for Christ, but Paul was the one prisoner whose bondage preserved the rights of Gentile Christians to be accepted without keeping the law of Moses.
4. Paul had first been arrested in Jerusalem by those Jews who opposed his accepting Gentiles into the church without making them keep the ceremonies of the Law. They accused him of bringing Gentiles into the temple (Acts 21:28), and they

refused to listen to him speak about the Gentiles (Acts 22:21-22).

5. If Paul had not been true to the message revealed to him, many Gentiles would have been deceived and forced into keeping the ceremonies of the law of Moses. But Paul closed his mouth in our defence, not even to avoid imprisonment. Thus his imprisonment was "in our behalf" (literally, "over" us), and it shielded us from an unbearable and unnecessary yoke being placed on our necks.

We ought to be like Paul, ever ready to stand up and speak out for the truth, regardless of personal consequences.

Fact Questions

132. Why was Paul originally arrested?
133. What could have happened to the Gentiles if Paul had been silent, and not submitted to imprisonment?

Text (3:2, 3)

2 If so be that ye have heard of the dispensation of that grace of God which was given me to you-ward; 3 how that by revelation was made known unto me the mystery, as I wrote before in few words

Thought Questions (3:2-3)

126. Could Paul have written to people as well known to him as the Ephesians, and said, "if ye have heard of the dispensation of the grace of God which was given to me"?
127. How did Paul get the message which he preached?
128. What meaning did the word *mystery* have to the Gentiles?
129. In what sense is Christianity a mystery?
130. To what does Paul refer when he said, "as I wrote before in few words"?

Paraphrase

2. Assuming, of course, that you have heard of that stewardship (management) of the message of God's grace, which was given to me to deliver unto you;

3. How that there has been made known unto me by revelation of God the mystery, that previously unknown sacred secret, as I have written previously in this epistle in a few words. (Compare 1:9.)

Notes (3:2-3)

1. "If ye have heard" is a simple conditional expression, eige-akousate, used when one wished to assume that what he said was true. We could also translate it, "For you must have heard . . . " or, "Assuming that you have heard . . . " Therefore the statement does not indicate that the writer was writing to people who were strangers to him. Paul could have written these words to the Ephesians as properly as to anyone else. (Compare the notes on 1:15.)

   Another thought on the phrase, "if ye have heard," is this: Paul's work while he was at Ephesus became known to all the province of Asia (Acts 19:10, 17). Some of the people in outlying areas from Ephesus may have heard of Paul and the Jesus whom he preached, but may not have heard how Paul had been entrusted to bring the Gospel to the Gentiles. Paul therefore explains about his ministry in this section, so that everyone might know clearly about it.

2. Paul began his prayer for us at verse one. As he began his prayer, he mentioned that he was the prisoner of Christ in behalf of us Gentiles. The reference to this fact diverted his prayer for a moment, as he launched into a parenthetical explanation of how God had given him the work of preaching to the Gentiles. Paul resumed the prayer at verse 14. Note that 3:1 and 3:14 begin with the same words.

3. A *dispensation* is a stewardship, or administration, or management of a household. Christ revealed to Paul much truth. Paul was a good manager and worker with the truth and "dispensed" the message faithfully.

4. As 3:2 indicates, the Christian Gospel is basically a message of grace (see notes on 1:6 and 2:8). God loved us when we were yet sinners. God accepts us now, not because we deserve it, but as a favor bestowed upon us by His love. Without Jesus as an advocate, our filthy souls could not stand in God's presence for one second.

5. Paul preached a message that had been revealed directly to him from God. Paul had no contact with the other apostles for several years after his conversion. He never had much contact with them (see Galatians, chapter 1). But he preached the same message that they did, for Christ revealed the same Gospel to all.

   We must accept Paul's words as inspired and coming directly from Christ (compare I Corinthians 14:37 and

Galatians 1:11-12). Many people try to belittle Paul's writings as if they were the personal opinions of some soured old bachelor or epileptic fanatic. We dare not think such thoughts.

6. Much is said in Ephesians about the *mystery* of Christ (see 1:9; 3:3, 4, 9; 5:32; 6:19).

    The New Testament uses the term *mystery* 27 times, mostly in Paul's writings. It is applied to several hidden, or once-hidden, or deep truths.

    The Gentiles were familiar with mystery religions. When people were initiated into some cult, they were told the mysteries or secret teachings of the cult. The Greeks had their Elusian and Orphic mysteries. The Persians had Mithraism, and the Egyptians the mysteries of Isis and Serapis. The religion of Diana had its mysteries.

    Here in Ephesians the mystery referred to is the fact which was formerly unknown, but is now revealed, that the Gentiles have equal privileges with the Jews (see 3:6). This was the sacred secret unknown in former ages, but now revealed and publicized to all men.

    Thus in the New Testament the word *mystery* is used in its ancient sense of a *revealed secret,* and not in its modern sense of that which cannot be fathomed or comprehended. There is nothing mysterious or hidden about the Gospel, even if there are deep things in it. It is called a mystery only because at one time it was not made known to the sons of men.

7. That which Paul had written "before in a few words" may either refer to some previous writing of Paul which the Ephesians had seen, or to what Paul had written previously in this letter about the mystery of Christ (1:9-10). The latter idea seems much more likely, because Paul's writings were not then generally circulated around as they are now.

Fact Questions

134. How else have we translated the phrase "if ye have heard"?
135. What are some words that mean the same as *dispensation*?
136. By what means was the mystery made known to Paul?
137. Why is the gospel called a *mystery*?
138. What is a reason for thinking that what Paul had written "before in few words" refers to previous remarks in this letter?

Text (3:4)

4 whereby, when ye read, ye can perceive my understanding in the mystery of Christ

Thought Questions (3:4)

131. Can we expect God to put His truths directly into our minds and lips?

132. What are we to read to find out the whole truth about the will of God?

Paraphrase

4. Concerning this mystery that was revealed to me, when ye read what I have written, you shall be able to grasp my perfect understanding of the matter.

Notes (3:4)

1. We cannot expect to receive information directly from God into our mind and speech, as Paul did. Paul did not tell us to pray for such enlightenment, but to READ what he had written, for God had given to him perfect understanding of the matter.

   Some people think that they will always know the truth because they pray for the Holy Spirit to guide them. They should go and read what the Spirit told Paul and the apostles once for all. The only spirit likely to guide us without studying is some "seducing spirit" (I Timothy 4:1).

2. It has been suggested that the phrase, "when ye read," may refer to reading the Old Testament. Paul sometimes proved the truth of his preaching by appealing to the Old Testament for support (Acts 17:2, 11). Paul's message brought to light many hidden truths of the Old Testament.

   Even so, the natural and obvious thing suggested by "when ye read" is that it has reference to reading Paul's own writings.

3. Only when we read (or "know accurately") the writings of the *apostles* will we have infallible divine information. We cannot get divine truth from the great or wise men of this world.

4. Concerning the *mystery,* see notes on 3:2-3, 6.

Fact Questions

139. What must we do to perceive Paul's understanding of the mystery of Christ?
140. Should we depend upon the Holy Spirit to give us direct enlightenment concerning the mystery of Christ?

Text (3:5)

5 which in other generations was not made known unto the sons of men, as it hath now been revealed unto his holy apostles and prophets in the Spirit

Thought Questions (3:5)

133. Did Abraham and Moses and other Old Testament saints know of God's plan for salvation?
134. Why did God put off so long the revealing of His mystery of salvation to the world?
135. How much of our knowledge of God's will do we owe to the prophets?

Paraphrase

5. The mystery of Christ was not made known to men in the ages before the apostles, as it has now been made known directly by the Holy Spirit to the holy apostles of Christ and the prophets of New Testament times.

Notes

1. "In other generations" refers to the ages or generations of mankind who lived before the church began on Pentecost A.D. 33 (A.D. 29 according to our calendars). Neither Confucius, nor Buddha, nor the philosophers knew what God has now revealed, and their disciples still do not know it.

Abraham, Moses, and other Old Testament saints did not know the mystery of Christ, "God having provided some better thing for us, that without us they should not be made perfect" (Hebrews 11:40). God accepted these men because He knew that Christ would shed His blood for all men later. But this way of salvation was unknown to them. Even the prophets who predicted the coming of Christ did not understand the prophecies they uttered (I Peter 1:10-12). Their messages remained a mystery until Christ had died and rose again, and the Holy Spirit revealed the meaning of all these things to the apostles. Note the emphasis on the fact that

the mystery is NOW revealed to the holy apostles and
prophets.

2. It was the Holy Spirit that revealed the mystery of Christ to
the apostles and prophets. On the day of Pentecost the
apostles spoke as the Spirit gave them utterance (compare II
Peter 1:21). At other times when they spoke or wrote, the
Holy Spirit gave them thoughts and words (I Corinthians
2:10-13).

3. The prophets referred to here are the New Testament
prophets, such as Silas, Agabus, etc. (see Acts 11:27-28;
13:1; 15:32; Ephesians 2:20). These men spoke the message
of God, for God put it directly into their minds and mouths.

Not much information is given in the Bible concerning
the New Testament prophets. In Ephesians Paul sets a very
high estimate on their work. It may be that more of our
knowledge of the way of life has come to us through the
prophets than we realize.

Fact Questions

141. To what two groups of men has God revealed the mystery
of Christ?

142. In (or by) what has the mystery been revealed?

Text (3:6)

6 *to wit*, that the Gentiles are fellow-heirs, and fellow-members of the body, and fellow-partakers of the promise in Christ
Jesus through the gospel

Thought Questions (3:6)

136. What is the standing of the Gentiles in the church compared
to that of the Jews?

137. How many churches are the Jews and Gentiles to form?

138. What will we inherit as "fellow-heirs" of God? (See
Matthew 19:29; 25:34.)

Paraphrase

6. The mystery which was revealed to me is, in brief, the
revelation that the Gentiles are now equal in privileges with
the Jews, and that when both are saved through Christ, they
are heirs of God together, members of the one body (church)
together, and partakers together of the promise of the Messiah, through the gospel of Christ Jesus.

Notes (3:6)

1. The expressions, "fellow-heirs," "fellow-members," and "fellow partakers," as given in the American Standard Version (quoted above) are a splended attempt to reproduce in English the alliteration of this verse in Greek. Each of the Greek words translated as given above begins with the same syllable, a prefix meaning "together" or "with."

2. Most Jews felt that if the Gentiles were ever accepted of God, it would only be when they became subject to the law of Moses. The revelation that both Jews and Gentiles stand on equal footing with God through Christ was more than many zealous Hebrew Christians would accept (Acts 15:5).

3. Christ has only one body, one church. Jews and Gentiles are fellow-members of the one body. Denominational divisions, social or racial divisions in the church are not of God's making, and are not pleasing to Him.

4. We are fellow-partakers of THE promise. One great promise runs throughout the Old Testament, and gave hope to all the ages before Christ. That was the promise of the Messiah. This promise had many shining aspects to it, like the facets of a diamond. But it was a single promise.

   This promise has now been fulfilled, and lo! the Gentiles are made to share in the benefits of it through the Gospel (which is the death, burial, and resurrection of Christ (I Corinthians 15:1-4). The spiritual condition of our ancestors before Christ was so dreadful that we really ought to thank God for being made fellow-partakers of the promise. (Compare Ephesians 2:11-12.)

Fact Questions

143. Name the three things in which the Gentiles are now "fellows" with the Jews.

144. What was the promise of which the Gentiles are made fellow-partakers?

145. Ephesians 3:6 defines the content of what?

Text (3:7)

7 whereof I was made a minister, according to the gift of that grace of God which was given me, according to the working of his power.

Thought Questions (3:7)

139. Of what was Paul made a minister?
140. Why would God choose a murderer, blasphemer, and persecutor like Paul to be His minister?
141. How did God's power work in the life of Paul?

Paraphrase

7. Of the gospel, I Paul was made minister (or servant). This ministry was given to me as a gracious gift of God, and God empowered me with miraculous powers by the working of His power to accomplish my ministry.

Notes (3:7)

1. "Whereof" refers to the Gospel, mentioned in 3:6. Of this gospel Paul was made a minister.

2. The word *minister* used here is the same term (*diakonos*) that is elsewhere translated *servant, attendant,* or *deacon.* We can be a *minister* of God and serve Him as a *minister* in many ways. "He that is greatest among you shall be your servant (minister)" (Matthew 23:11).

3. The two phrases (1) "according to the gift of that grace of God which was given me," and (2) "according to the working of his power," seem to be parallel, and both describe the ministry of Paul. The idea is that Paul's ministry was not self-chosen (it was a gift to him), and was not dependent upon his own natural ability for its success.

4. Because Paul had been a blasphemer, a persecutor, and injurious before his conversion (I Timothy 1:12-13), he felt especially indebted to God after his conversion, and tried to make up for all his years of opposing Christ. Sometimes the greatest sinners, when converted, will serve Christ the most earnestly and gratefully. Even so, Paul would never have been chosen as a minister unless God had seen fit to bestow that ministry as a gift of His grace (favor).

5. The "working" of God's power enabled Paul to work miracles, speak by prophetic inspiration, and guided him into great, marvelous, and hard service. Any sincere servant of God today will find that God leads and helps him in a powerful and marvelous way, even if we do not have the miraculous gifts such as Paul had.

Fact Questions

146. According to what two things was Paul made a minister?

Text (3:8, 9)

8 Unto me, who am less than the least of all saints, was this grace given, to preach unto the Gentiles the unsearchable riches of Christ; and to make all men see what is the dispensation of the mystery which for ages hath been hid in God who created all things;

Thought Questions (3:8-9)

142. How could anyone be less than the least of saints?
143. What are the unsearchable riches of Christ? If you do not know, how can you preach what Paul preached?
144. What is the dispensation of the mystery which Paul was to make all men see?
145. Why did God hide His program from so many ages?

Paraphrase

8. Unto me, Paul, who am inferior to even the least distinguished of the saints because I persecuted the church, to me was this favor given to preach to the Gentiles the riches of Christ, which are so vast that they are unsearchable, beyond tracing out in their fullness;

9. and I am appointed to enlighten all men concerning the present Christian age (or dispensation), the knowledge of which has been hidden from the people who have lived in previous ages, hidden within the mind of God who created all things.

Notes (3:8-9)

1. Things may be little, less, or least. But Paul sincerely considered himself less than the least of saints in personal merit. Concerning the "saints," see the notes on Ephesians 1:1.

2. Paul had always been sincere, even when sincerely mistaken (Acts 24:16). He was highly educated. He was earnest in his work. He had high moral character. In spite of all of these good things, he was a great sinner before his conversion. In fact, he was the chief of sinners (I Timothy 1:15), and less than the least of saints.

    Paul's testimony should be a stern warning to those who are self-righteous, and pride themselves on being good moral men. We can be the chief of sinners in spite of morality.

3. The low estimate that Paul places upon himself in 3:8 excludes the possibility that this epistle could have been

written by some admiring disciple of Paul's (such as Onesimus) in Paul's name. Some modern commentaries actually teach that very thing.

4. The "grace" given to Paul was his ministry, the same as that "gift of grace" referred to in 3:7. Paul should have been put to death for opposing Christ. Instead, God graciously appointed him to be an honored minister.

5. Paul was recognized and accepted by the other apostles as being divinely sent to the Gentiles (Galatians 2:9).

6. The early Christians had the unsearchable riches of Christ. Few had social standings, few had material wealth, yet they were filled with joy and radiant love. What were these riches of Christ which they had?

When you consider what these early disciples had, it actually amounts to a few intangible blessings, such as:
(1) Fellowship with Christ
(2) Fellowship with one another
(3) Assurance of pardon from sin
(4) Assurance of eternal life
(5) Assurance that they knew the truth
(6) The Holy Spirit within them

Would these intangible blessings satisfy our modern church members, who have to be entertained, coddled, flattered, babied, and tricked into being faithful? These need to learn the preciousness of being in Christ, the joy of Christian fellowship (I John 1:3), the joy of the Holy Spirit (I Thessalonians 1:6).

A Christian who is so in love with Jesus that he can say,

"Sun of my soul, thou savior dear,
It is not night when thou art near;
O may no earth-born cloud arise
To hide thee from thy servant's eyes"

truly has grasped some of the "riches of Christ."

7. The riches of Christ are not called *unsearchable* because they are confusing or vague, but because they are so vast that no human can trace out all the priceless aspects and phrases of them.

8. The word *fellowship* of the King James Version (3:9) is correctly replaced by *dispensation* (or *stewardship*) in the Revised Version.

9. The phrase, "by Christ Jesus" in the Authorized Version (3:9) is not in the best Greek texts and is omitted by the

Revised Version. It is absolutely true that God created the universe through Christ, and for Christ (John 1:3; Colossians 1:16), but that fact is not stated in this text.

10. Concerning the "mystery," see notes on 3:3, 6.

11. During the times before Christ came, God tolerated the nations on earth to walk in their own ways, and He over-looked those times of ignorance (Acts 14:16; 17:30). But now God wants to make all men see (enlighten them concerning) the present dispensation of the mystery. People must know that God now commands all men everywhere to repent and obey the Gospel.

12. For ages (literally "from the ages" (compare Colossians 1:26) the mystery of God's will had been hidden in God, that is, in the mind and plan of God. We might ask, "Why did God wait so long to reveal His mystery, when the world needed it so greatly?" We cannot know God's reasons for doing things. But it is evident to everyone that by the time that God revealed His mystery, the world had fully discovered that it could not save itself by philosophy, law, military might, or any other human means. Hence, the world should have been fully ready to receive Christ.

Fact Questions

147. How did Paul compare himself to other saints?
148. To whom was Paul sent to preach?
149. What was Paul to preach, according to 3:8?
150. What was Paul to make all men see (3:9)?
151. Where had the mystery been hidden?

Text (3:10)

10 to the intent that now unto the principalities and the powers in the heavenly *places* might be made known through the church the manifold wisdom of God,

Thought Questions (3:10)

146. What are the "principalities and powers" to which God's wisdom is to be made known?
147. Are there good and bad angels and spiritual beings all around us?
148. What is Satan's opinion of God's efforts to save us?
149. Where and how can we show to the principalities and powers that God is wise?
150. What kind of wisdom is "manifold" wisdom?

Paraphrase

10. Not only was I made a minister to make known the present administration of God's program to men, but also that the manifold wisdom of God might now be made known to the angelic hosts, the first rulers and authorities (both good and evil) who dwell in the heavenly regions of the air; this wisdom is made known to them through the church, for the church testifies by its existence that God did not send Christ in vain.

Notes (3:10)

1. All about us are unseen hosts of angelic beings and spirit creatures. We cannot see them but, like Elisha's servant (II Kings 6:15-17), we could if God opened our eyes.

   The devil and his angels are here on earth (Revelation 12:12), inhabiting the region of the air (Ephesians 2:2), which is called the "heavenly places." They go about looking for anyone whom they may devour (I Peter 5:8).

   The devil apparently has his forces organized into an efficient army, with ranks of authority and work assigned. We, as Christians, wrestle not against flesh and blood (human enemies), but against the principalities, against the powers, against the world rulers of this darkness, against the spiritual hosts of wickedness in the heavenly places (Ephesians 6:12). These "principalities and powers" thus seem to refer to high-ranking evil angels in the army of Satan. "Principalities and powers" may be translated "first rulers and authorities."

2. Many modernist scholars deny the existence of spirit beings such as the "principalities and powers." One modern writer says that it is not necessary or even possible for us to return to this ancient way of thinking about the spiritual forces that inhabit our universe. People with opinions like that will have their eyes opened, but probably too late.

3. Satan, whose every thought is evil, cannot believe that any person would serve God without selfish interests. To Satan's mind, God's efforts to save man are foolishness and can be thwarted.

   Once God asked Satan, "Have you considered my servant Job?" (Job 1:8). Satan had indeed observed that Job served God faithfully, and that God had blessed him with abundant wealth. So Satan replied to God, "Doth Job fear God for nought? — put forth thy hand now, and touch all that he hath, and he will renounce thee to thy face" (Job 1:9-11). God allowed Job to be tested, and Job lost everything that he had. But when Job remained faithful in spite of all this loss, it proved that Satan was wrong about Job, and that God was wise in blessing him.

4. Likewise, God makes His wisdom known at the present time to the principalities and powers through the CHURCH. Faithful church members are a constant testimony that God was wise in sending His Son to die for us. God can say to the devil, "In spite of all your lies and temptations, these people in the church have accepted My Son Jesus as Lord and Savior. This proves I was wise to send Christ to die for them."

Question — Are you a church member, proving to Satan that God was wise in offering salvation to you? Or does the devil gloat because you refuse to serve Christ in the church?

5. Not only the evil angels, but the angels of God as well, are deeply interested in God's plan of salvation. During those ages when the mystery of salvation was yet unrevealed, the angels "desired to look into" these matters (I Peter 1:12). Surely it was hard for them to understand how a just and holy God, who was too pure to behold iniquity, could pardon and accept sinful men, who were under the just sentence of eternal death. But now these angels can see the wisdom of God demonstrated in the church made up of men pardoned through the blood of Christ.

6. Thus our faith is not a private matter, but is bound up with God's purpose for the whole universe.

7. God's wisdom is manifold. It has many forms, various objectives, efforts, many methods and means, and is unsearchable by human minds (Romans 11:33). It is many-splendored.

Fact Questions

152. What are the principalities and powers in the heavenly places?

153. Through what is the wisdom of God made known to the principalities and powers?

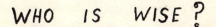

Text (3:11, 12)

11 according to the eternal purpose which he purposed in Christ Jesus our Lord: 12 in whom we have boldness and access in confidence through our faith in him.

Thought Questions (3:11-12)

151. Has God permitted the universe and man to develop as chance and time might cause and direct?

152. Who is the central character in God's eternal plan?

153. Should we not approach a holy and just God with fear and trembling?

154. How can we who are sinful, disobedient souls have opportunity to come into the presence of the almighty God?

Paraphrase

11. This work of showing God's wisdom to the principalities and powers is part of and according to God's eternal purpose and program, which he has made in Christ, that is, with Christ as its center, object, and means.

12. In Christ, around whom God's eternal purpose was made, we miserable sinners may have boldness in approaching God, and an open, clear access (way of approach) unto Him. And we have this access not through meritorious works that we have done, but through faith in Christ.

Notes (3:11-12)

1. God's intention of showing His wisdom to the evil angelic powers is according to an eternal purpose which He had made. God's purpose (*prothesis,* plan, or pre-planned program) was made before the world began, and cannot be overthrown. The wisdom of God will overcome the sin, greed, lust, war, meanness, and weeping of our sin-cursed world.

2. It was the work of Satan that caused man to sin, suffer, and die back at the beginning. God, foreseeing that this would happen, determined before the foundation of the world that Christ should suffer, die, and rise again, and thus bring to nought the power of the Devil. (See Ephesians 1:4.) God is still directing the course of human events in order to accomplish His will. Even the wrath of men shall ultimately praise Him (Psalm 76:10; Ephesians 1:10-11).

3. In Christ Jesus we have boldness to come unto the Father. *Boldness* here means *freedom in all speaking.* We may come to God in prayer boldly. But only in Christ can we have such boldness.

We generally take too much for granted about our own merits, rights, and privileges. We do not fear God as He ought to be feared because of His greatness, holiness, and power. We would not crash into the room where a king or president was working. But we often approach the Lord of all the universe with a reckless and demanding attitude. Let us not forget that it is a fearful thing to fall into the hands of the living God (Hebrews 10:31). He is God, and we are only flesh.

Nonetheless, THROUGH JESUS CHRIST we can come to the Father with boldness. Unlike the heathen who are afraid of their gods, we come to God with boldness. But let us come with reverential boldness, not with impudence, reckless demands, and irreverence.

4. In Christ Jesus we not only have boldness, but access to the Father. Paul mentioned this access in 2:18. An *access* is a way of approach or an introduction. We cannot speak to a government official without proper introductions being made through the right people. Christ gives us access to the Father. We have no goodness in ourselves to demand such an access, and no power to command or force an access to the Father.

5. Our access to God through Christ is used with confidence through "the faith of him" (Christ). We do not deserve such an honor as free access to God, but God has graciously granted it to us simply through the faith we have in Christ. Compare the notes on 2:8.

Fact Questions

154. What is it that is referred to as being "according to the eternal purpose" of God?
155. In Whom did God make His eternal purpose?
156. In Whom can we have boldness in approaching the Father?
157. What is an *access?*
158. Through what does our confidence in approaching God come?

Text (3:13)

13 wherefore I ask that ye may not faint at my tribulations for you, which are your glory.

Thought Questions (3:13)

155. Was Paul more concerned about himself or his brethren?
156. What evil effects could the sufferings of Paul have had on the other Christians?
157. How could Paul's sufferings be our glory?

Paraphrase

13. Wherefore, on account of all the honors given unto me in my ministry, I ask that you Ephesians not be disheartened and faint because of my troubles in prison for asserting your title to the riches of Christ. For my tribulations are your glory, a credit to every member of the church of Christ with which church I am identified.

Notes (3:13)

1. "Faint" here means to do evil, draw or shrink back in battle, be weary, or lose courage. The Ephesians could have become discouraged because of sympathy and fellow-feeling with Paul in his sufferings. Or they could have fainted out of fear that they would soon be enduring the same miseries that Paul was enduring.

2. Paul's tribulations were "for you", the Gentiles. He was in prison for defending their rights to the riches of Christ. See notes on 3:1.

3. It is indeed a glory to us that Paul suffered as he did. His victories in suffering made the whole church of Christ with which he was identified appear honorable. Likewise, when we suffer for Christ without surrendering to evil, it is a glory to all our fellow church members.

4. We observe in Paul's request that the Ephesians not faint at his tribulations the apex of Christian courtesy and consideration for others. Paul, the prisoner, was concerned about the free disciples, hoping that his tribulations were not causing THEM to stumble.

Fact Questions

159. What did Paul ask the Ephesians not to do because of his tribulations?
160. For whom were Paul's tribulations?
161. What did Paul say that his tribulations were to the Ephesians?

Text (3:14, 15)

14 For this cause, I bow my knees unto the Father, 15 from whom every family in heaven and on earth is named

Thought Questions (3:14-15)

158. For what cause was it that Paul bowed his knees to the Father?
159. If God's family is both in heaven and on earth, and they are all named from Him, what is their name?

Paraphrase

14. For this cause of which I began to speak before digressing off onto the subject of my ministry, namely that Christ has made both Jews and Gentiles into one temple, one body (2:15-22), I Paul do bow my knees in prayer unto the father,

15. From whom (the Father) the whole family of God's created beings in heaven and on earth is named; unto Him do I pray for you brethren.

Notes (3:14-15)

1. In this verse (14) Paul resumes the prayer that he began at 3:1, which was interrupted by the parenthetical discussion of his ministry (3:2-13).

2. "For this cause" refers to the glorious fact that the Gentiles are now accepted as fellow-citizens and are made into one temple of God with the Jews (see 2:11-22). It was for that cause that Paul prayed. Paul prayed, not just when there was trouble, but out of gratitude over the doctrines of Christ.

3. Paul bowed his knees unto the Father when he prayed. We need to limber up our spiritual arthritis and bend our knees unto God more often. Men do not bend the knees until they have first bent their pride.

4. Probably the translation in the King James Version, "the *whole* family in heaven and earth," is preferable to that in the Revised Version given above, "*every* family in heaven and on earth." God has only one family.

   The word *family* used here means "a race, or tribe, or family lineage going back to a common father; a fatherhood." Every human being on earth has descended from Adam, who is called the "son of God" (Luke 3:38). In the sense that we all owe our existence to God's creation, we may

95

all be called "sons of God," and thus we are named from God. Of course, if we commit sin, we become children of the Devil. (See John 8:44.)

5. The angels of God are also called the "sons of God" (Job 1:6; 38:7). They may be the ones described as the "family in heaven" who are named from the Father.

But it may be that the "family in heaven" refers to the saints of God who have died and are now with the Father in heaven.

6. "The name of *Father* has not gone up from us, but has come to us from above; for it is manifest that God is Father by nature, and not only in name." (Severian) It is absolutely true, as Alexander Campbell contended in his debate with Robert Owen, that man could never have conceived the idea of a supreme God unless God had revealed Himself to man. We have not given the name *Father* to some idea of a supreme power. The name of *Father* has been taught to us by the Father Himself through His Son Jesus (Matthew 6:9).

Fact Questions

162. What is this section (3:1, 14-19) called in the outline?
163. Where did Paul begin the prayer which he picked up again at 3:14?
164. In what physical position did Paul pray?
165. From Whom is every family in heaven and on earth named?
166. What two interpretations of the phrase, "the family in heaven," are given in the notes?

Text (3:16-19)

16 that he would grant you, according to the riches of his glory, that ye may be strengthened with power through his Spirit in the inward man; 17 that Christ may dwell in your hearts by faith; to the end that ye, being rooted and grounded in love, 18 may be strong to apprehend with all the saints what is the breadth and length and height and depth, 19 and to know the love of Christ which passeth knowledge; that ye may be filled unto all the fulness of God.

Thought Questions (3:16-19)

160. How great are the riches of God's glory?
161. If God's grant of strength is given according to the riches of His glory, how greatly should we expect to be strengthened?

162. Do we have any good excuse for letting sin defeat us when God strengthens us according to the riches of His glory?

163. Through what does God strengthen us with power?

164. What is a person's *inward man*?

165. By what does Christ dwell in our hearts (v. 17)? Through Whom does Christ dwell in the Christian, according to John 14:16-18?

166. In what is the Christian to take root?

167. What does Christ dwelling in our hearts have to do with our being rooted and grounded in love?

168. What do you think is meant by the "breadth and length and height and depth" of the gospel?

169. What is likely to happen if the child of God does not comprehend the true greatness of the gospel?

170. How can we know the love of Christ if it passes knowledge?

171. How much of the divine fulness can we humans here and now expect to receive?

Paraphrase

16. Praying that the Father would grant you, in a manner according to the great riches of His glory, that you may be mightily strengthened through the indwelling of the Holy Spirit in your inward man, so that you will have the necessary strength to live as you ought to live.

17. Praying also a second request, that Christ may dwell in your hearts to the greatest possible degree as a result of the increasing faith which you have in Him.

    And (a third request that you, being rooted in love, as a tree is rooted, and well-founded upon love, as a sturdy building with a good foundation —

18. that you may have such full strength of spiritual discernment that you will be able to comprehend, along with all other saints, the surpassing breadth and length and height and depth of the Christian faith,

19. that indeed you may know the love of Christ, which is so great that it exceeds mere human knowledge without divine strengthening.

    As a climactic fourth request, I pray that you may be filled unto all the fulness of the divine power, love, and favor which God himself bestows upon his saints.

Notes (3:16-19)

PAUL'S REQUEST FOR US

1. That we be strengthened through God's Spirit. 3:16.
2. That Christ dwell in our hearts. 3:17.
3. That we be able to comprehend the breadth, length, height and depth. 3:18.
4. That we be filled unto all the fulness of God. 3:19.

DO YOU EVER PRAY FOR THESE THINGS?

1. The phrase, "riches of his glory," is a favorite expression of Paul (Ephesians 1:18; Philippians 4:19; Romans 9:23; Colossians 1:27; etc.). The fact that it is used here in Ephesians is further proof that Paul actually wrote Ephesians, and that the epistle is not a forgery under Paul's name, as some have dared to teach.

2. The riches from which God can supply us with all things are too great for humans to measure. God's riches are of every kind, material and spiritual. If God strengthens us according to HIS riches, through HIS Spirit, surely we shall be powerful enough to conquer every temptation and serve Christ victoriously.

   The phrase "strengthened with power" simply means "mightily strengthened."

3. The "inward man" refers to the non-material part of our being, our spirit, conscience, mind, and emotions. The term "inward man" is used in Romans 7:22 to describe that spiritual part of our nature that delights in God's law, contrasted to that fleshly part of our makeup which craves sin. The "inward man" is mentioned in II Corinthians 4:16. "Though our outward man (the physical body) perish, yet the inward man is renewed day by day."

   It is much more important that the inward man be strengthened than the outward man, even though it is necessary to be strong physically. People can do much for God even in great suffering, weakness, and poverty if they are strong inwardly.

4. Christ dwells in us through the Holy Spirit (John 14:16-18, 23). Our faith is the entrance through which Christ enters. Our faith in Christ ought to grow stronger and stronger as we serve Christ. Then as our faith grows stronger, Christ

will dwell in us in a greater way through the Holy Spirit and the Word of God.

5. The verb *dwell* (*katoikeo*) means "to settle or dwell permanently," contrasted to a related verb (*paroikeo*) meaning to "sojourn or dwell temporarily." Christ is to dwell in our hearts to stay.

6. *Grounded* means "having a foundation" or "made stable." We are to be rooted as a sturdy tree and founded as a temple with solid foundations.

7. We are rooted and grounded "in love." Love is the soil into which we are rooted, and the solid earth upon which we are founded. Unless our work and faith is rooted and grounded in love, it is no good.

   Being rooted and grounded in love comes as a result of Christ dwelling in our hearts through faith.

8. The average Christian does not grasp the greatness of His salvation. We need to pray that all may comprehend the breadth, length, height, and depth. Unless they do, they are liable to backslide.

   Of course Christianity is not reduceable to certain mathematical dimensions — height, depth, length, breadth. This is a rhetorical expression used to express vividly the great fulness of our salvation.

9. To "know the love of Christ" is part of comprehending the breadth, length, height, and depth. This love of Christ actually passes knowledge. It cannot be described by words, or pictures, or human expression. This knowledge develops by long experience with Christ, by study of His Word, and by prayer. As we walk with Him, and repeatedly see His power and mercy, we come more and more to know the love that passes knowledge.

10. The clause "that you may be filled unto all the fulness of God," is coordinate with the clauses in 3:16, 18, being likewise introduced by *hina*. We have made this more evident in the text by changing the comma after *knowledge* to a semicolon. Note the outline of chapter three.

11. The thought that we may be filled unto all the fulness of God may be a bit staggering. (Concerning *fulness*, see the notes on 1:23.) However, the expression does not mean that we may expect to become like God in power and sinlessness.

However, we can, and need to be filled with all the fulness of sincerity, love of God, mercy, firmness for the right, kindness, etc., which God has provided for us to have. This degree of fulness is far beyond what most of us seek for. Too often we are content to play along the shore of God's sea of blessings. We have too low an opinion of what God can do for us, and what we can be and do. Oftentimes we do not want to launch out into the deep. We love the shallows where few demands are made upon our talents, will power, and energy.

Fact Questions

167. What were Paul's four petitions for the Ephesians?
168. Paul prayed that God would grant the Ephesians to be strengthened according to what?
169. Through what are we strengthened with power?
170. What is the means through which Christ dwells in us?
171. In what are we to be rooted and grounded?
172. Name the four dimensions of the Christian faith in the order given.
173. What is it that passes knowledge?
174. To what degree are we to be filled?

Text (3:20, 21)

20 Now unto him that is able to do exceeding abundantly above all that we ask or think, according to the power that worketh in us, 21 unto him *be* the glory in the church and in Christ Jesus unto all generations forever and ever. Amen.

Thought Questions (3:20-21)

173. Who is it that is able to exceeding abundantly above all that we ask or think?
174. How much can you think of for God to do? Can God do that much? Can He do more than that?
175. Is God's power available to us now, or will it only be available to us in the future life?
176. What is ascribed to God?
177. In what two areas is God glorified? How is He glorified in each?
178. How long shall glory be ascribed to God?

Paraphrase

To paraphrase this sublime doxology is almost like trying to beautify a pear by painting it. Memorize it. Meditate on it. Make it your own.

Notes (3:20-21)

1. This sublime doxology comes at the close of an exalted prayer. The doxology informs us in moving words that our glorious God is able to grant the marvelous requests stated in the prayer of 3:16-19.
2. The word *doxology* means a "word of glory, or an ascription of glory." This definition certainly described these verses.
3. God not only can do great things, but He can do exceeding abundantly (or beyond all measure) above all things which we can ask or think. We can think of great things for God to do. God can do much more than we ask or think that it is beyond all measure.
4. This unimaginable ability of God is "according to the power" that "doth energize itself" within us (Rotherham). God's power is working within us now. We do not have to wait until the future life to avail ourselves of it.
5. God is glorified in the church and in Christ Jesus. In the church, God is glorified as His saints praise Him and His saving grace. Also, God is glorified in the church because the very fact of its existence causes heavenly beings to glorify God for redeeming such a body unto Himself (Revelation 5:8-10).

   God is glorified in Christ Jesus because Christ did always do His Father's will, and glorify His Father's name (John 17:4). And the pleasure of the Lord prospers in His (Christ's) hand (Isaiah 53:10).
6. This glory unto God is to continue "unto all the generations of the age of the ages" (Revised Version, margin). Here, as elsewhere in the Scriptures, eternity is viewed not as one incomprehensibly endless period, but as a succession of ages, one after another, stretching as far as can be perceived, and then on beyond.

Fact Questions

175. How does this doxology fittingly close the prayer of 3:16-19?
176. Quote from memory the doxology and give its Scripture limitations.

THE SECOND HALF OF EPHESIANS

The second half of Ephesians is mostly exhortation to us to fulfill our DUTIES in the church. There are some passages of doctrine included (for example, 5:25-32), but it is primarily an exhortation to duties.

The first three chapters told of the glorious DOCTRINES of the church: our priceless blessings, the marvelous mystery of Christ, and other doctrines.

It is never enough merely to know and believe the doctrines of the church. We must obey and live by that which we learn. Paul, after telling us of the doctrines of the church at length, now says, "Therefore," and goes on to exhort us to do certain things. Ours is a "therefore" religion. God has given us many favors. THEREFORE we have certain responsibilities in return.

Previewing in Outline Form (4:1-6-20)

II. DUTIES — 4:1-6:20.
  A. Keep the unity of the Spirit. 4:1-16.
    1. Walk worthily of your calling. 4:1-3.
    2. Unity of the Spirit described. 4:4-6.
    3. Unity is served by a diversity of gifts. 4:7-16.
  B. Walk as becometh saints. 4:17-5:20.
    1. Walk not as the Gentiles walk. 4:17-24.
    2. Seven practical exhortations. 4:25-5:2.
    3. Walk as children of light. 5:3-14.
    4. Walk as wise men. 5:15-20.
  C. Subject yourselves one to another. 5:21-6:9.
    1. The command. 5:21.
    2. Wives and husbands. 5:22-33.
    3. Children and fathers. 6:1-4.
    4. Slaves and masters. 6:5-9.
  D. Put on the whole armor of God. 6:10-20.
    1. Exhortation to be strengthened. 6:10-13.
    2. The armor described. 6:14-17.
    3. Exhortation to prayer. 6:18-20.

Fact Questions

177. What is the word that describes the contents of the second half of Ephesians?

178. What are the four duties (A, B, C, D) listed in the outline? Give the Scripture limitations of each.

DUTIES

UNKNOWN AND NEGLECTED
BY MOST CHURCH MEMBERS

1. **KEEP THE UNITY OF THE SPIRIT,** Eph. 4:1-16

2. **WALK AS BECOMETH SAINTS,** Eph. 4:17-5:20

3. **SUBJECT YOURSELVES ONE TO ANOTHER,** Eph. 5:21-6:9

4. **PUT ON THE WHOLE ARMOR OF GOD,** Eph. 6:10-20

EPHESIANS FOUR

DUTIES OF CHURCH MEMBERS

1. **KEEP THE UNITY OF THE SPIRIT; 1-16**
   a. WALK WORTHILY, 1-3

   b. UNITY OF THE SPIRIT CONSISTS OF ONE BODY, SPIRIT, HOPE, LORD, FAITH, BAPTISM, GOD; 4-6

   c. UNITY AIDED BY A DIVERSITY OF GIFTS, 7-16

2. **WALK AS BECOMETH SAINTS: 4:17-5:20**

   a. WALK NOT AS GENTILES WALK
      (1) GENTILE WALK, 17-19
      (2) CHRISTIAN WALK, 20-24

   b. PRACTICAL EXHORTATIONS, 4:25-5:2

Previewing in Outline Form (4:1-16)

II. Duties. 4:1-6:20.
  A. Keep the unity of the Spirit. 4:1-16.
    1. Walk worthily of your calling. 4:1-3.
      a. With lowliness and meekness. 4:2.
      b. With longsuffering.
      c. Forbearing one another in love.
      d. Giving diligence to keep the unity of the Spirit. 4:3.
    2. Unity of the Spirit described. 4:4-6.

      a. One body.
      b. One Spirit.
      c. One hope.
      d. One Lord.
      e. One faith.
      f. One baptism.
      g. One God.

    3. Unity is served by a diversity of gifts. 4:7-16.
      a. Christ has given different gifts to each one. 4:7-11.
        (1) This is proved by a prophecy. 4:8-10.
        (2) The different gifts listed. 4:11.
      b. Purposes of the gifts. 4:12.
        (1) For the perfecting of the saints.
          — The perfected saints devote themselves to the work of ministering.
        (2) For the building up of the body of Christ.
      c. Objectives to be reached by the gifts. 4:13-16.
        (1) Unity of the faith and of the knowledge of the Son of God. 4:13.
        (2) Unto a fullgrown man.
        (3) Unto the measure of the stature of the fulness of Christ. 4:13-16.
          (a) We are not to remain children. 4:14.
            1 Children are tossed about.
            2 Children are carried about by every wind of doctrine.
          (b) We are to grow up into Christ. 4:15-16.
            1 Speaking the truth in love.
            2 Grow up in all things.

3 Christ is the head.
— From Christ all the body working
together makes the increase of the
body. 4:16.

Text (4:1)

I therefore, the prisoner in the Lord, beseech you to walk worthily of the calling wherewith ye were called.

Thought Questions (4:1)

179. Is it sufficient to know the doctrines of Christ, without living a transformed life?
180. What is the *walk* of a Christian?
181. What is God's *calling* by which we were called?
182. What type of a life is *worthy* of our calling?

Paraphrase

1. On account of the impelling force in the glorious doctrines of the church, I Paul, the prisoner in the Lord, exhort and beseech you to live in a manner that will be worthy of the gospel, that glorious calling by which you were called.

Notes (4:1)

1. Paul mentions that he was "the prisoner in the Lord." Paul was blessed (happy) in suffering. He was more blessed for being in bonds for the Lord's cause than for having once been caught up into Paradise (II Corinthians 12:3, 7). The word *prisoner* used here (and in 3:1) designates one in bonds.

2. Christian living is not done because a stern and specific law demands it. Rather, Paul beseeches (exhorts, or stands by calling) us to live the proper kind of life. The Law of God must be written in our hearts, not just on the law books. When it is written in our hearts, we will do the will of God even when we will not be seen by our fellow men.

3. Paul wanted us to marry "in the Lord" (I Corinthians 7:39), rejoice "in the Lord" (Philippians 3:1), and, if need be, to go to prison "in the Lord."

4. The adverb *worthily* comes from an adjective meaning "having the same weight; of like value." In the balances of life our *walk* (or daily manner of life) should be "of the same weight" as our calling. (Note the drawing on page 139.)

5. Our *calling* (or vocation) refers to the Gospel by which God has called us (II Thessalonians 2:14). Certainly the gospel

is good, noble, and undefiled. Our daily walk must be of like value with the Gospel by which we have been called. The Christian life is often described as a *walk* (Romans 6:4; II Corinthians 5:7; Galatians 5:16; Ephesians 2:2; Philippians 3:18; Colossians 1:10).

Fact Questions

179. By what are we called?
180. What is the walk of the Christian?
181. How is our walk to compare with our calling?

Text (4:2, 3)

2 with all lowliness and meekness, with longsuffering, forbearing one another in love; 3 giving diligence to keep the unity of the Spirit in the bond of peace.

Thought Questions (4:2-3)

183. Why shouldn't Christians have an attitude of superiority?
184. What does it mean to "forbear one another"?
185. How far should the Christian go in putting up with the shortcomings of others?
186. Can Christians have unity without working for it?
187. Are Christians to devise methods to produce unity, or to preserve the unity provided for them?
188. Can we have unity without peace?

Paraphrase

2. In order to live (or walk) in a manner worthy of our noble calling we must have a humble opinion of ourselves and a gentle disposition toward others. We need furthermore to exercise great patience in giving vent to anger, supporting one another in the miseries and shortcomings of life, because we are ruled by love and not by personal ambition;

3. Giving haste and attention as we seek to walk worthily, to keep that unity of the church which the Holy Spirit has provided. This unity can only be had when the members of the body are tied together by the bond of peace.

Notes (4:2-3)

1. These verses hint that personal differences and strains are constantly being felt within the church. Out in the world there are certainly strains, divisions, and contentions — nation against nation, capital against labor, race against race, north against south, etc. In the church, God is seeking to bring all things under *one* head, Christ (Ephesians 1:10). In order for this to be done, those in the church must be most careful about how they feel and act toward their brethren.

2. *Lowliness* is a humble opinion of oneself, a deep sense of moral littleness. We need this attitude because we are all sinful, and really know so very little.

3. *Meekness* is that characteristic and attitude that grows out of lowliness. It is mildness or gentleness. Meekness is not weakness. Moses was the meekest of men (Numbers 12:3), but he certainly was no "sissy."

4. *Longsuffering* is patience, control of anger, endurance, slowness in avenging wrongs.

5. *To forbear* is to hold up, sustain, or support. The attitude that we can push others down to exalt ourselves is not the attitude of love. We must forbear the shortcomings and imperfections of others, because we are ruled by love. We may teach, reprove, or correct those who have shortcomings, but in doing it, we need to demonstrate the patience and forbearance of love.

6. It is not easy to keep unity. We must *endeavor* (or, literally, give haste) to preserve it. It must be worked at. Unity is the design of God for all the universe (1:10; 2:15). Those who please God must promote unity.

7. However, we cannot create unity, nor methods of unity. A divine unity is granted to the church. When men are in Christ, they are automatically one with all others who are in Christ, unless they make divisions by joining denominations organized by men. Two souls who are in Christ will flow

together as two drops of water. They will have fellowship with one another unless some barrier is created between them. All barriers are of men, not of God.

There is nothing to be gained by creating councils of denominations. We are only to *keep or guard* the unity that has been supplied to the church by the Holy Spirit. We shun and oppose all human teachings, inventions, and denominations as being causes of division, stumbling, and discord.

8. "To divide the spiritual body of Christ is as cruel a crime against God and man as it is to pierce the fleshly body of Jesus with a spear." (David Lipscomb)

9. The "unity of the Spirit" is that unity which the Holy Spirit provided when He established the church. It is a Spirit-led kind of unity. When the church had this type of unity, it was all of one heart and soul (Acts 4:32).

10. The phrase, "unity of the Spirit," does not hint that there is some unseen spiritual unity between the divisions of the church. We cannot have spiritual unity when external divisions exist, for these divisions are evidence of a lack of internal unity. If unity is not visible, and cannot be demonstrated outwardly, it does not exist.

11. "In the bond of peace": A *bond* is something which binds together, a band. *Peace* is the bond which ties the unity of the Spirit together. It is not possible for unity to exist where there is enmity or discord. Nothing good can happen where fighting is going on (James 3:16, 18).

Fact Questions

182. What three characteristics must we have to walk worthily of our calling (v. 2)?

183. In what are we to forbear one another?

184. Describe the kind of unity indicated by the phrase "unity of the Spirit."

185. Is it necessary to invent methods of achieving unity? Why or why not?

186. In what bond are we to keep the unity of the Spirit?

NO UNITY POSSIBLE
UNLESS BOUND
TOGETHER BY
PEACE!

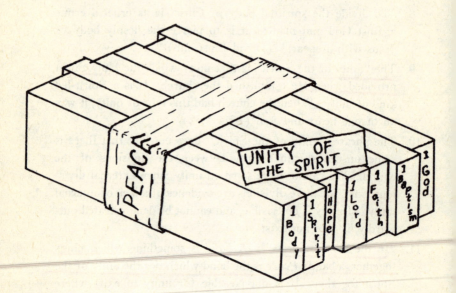

"Keep the
unity of the
Spirit in the
bond of peace."
Ephesians 4:3

Text (4:4)

4 There is one body, and one Spirit, even as also ye were called in one hope of your calling

Thought Questions (4:4)

189. What is the *one body*?
190. How should the fact that there is only "one body, one Spirit," etc., affect our relationships toward our brethren?
191. Does the *one hope* of the Christian consist of the hope of making this present world a better place?

Paraphrase

4. The "unity of the Spirit" which we are to keep consists of seven unities: (1) one body, the church of Christ; (2) one Spirit, the Holy Spirit; and, just as there is only one body and Spirit, so also (3) ye were called in only one hope of your calling. This one hope rests upon the grace that is to be brought to us when the Lord Jesus is revealed from heaven.

Notes (4:4)

1. Note that the words *there is* at the beginning of 4:4 are in italics, which indicates that they are not in the original Greek text, but are supplied into the English version for clarity and smoothness. Notice how verses three and four read when the *there is* is omitted: "Keep the unity of the Spirit in the bond of peace, one body, and one Spirit — " This plainly indicates that the unity of the Spirit consists in maintaining the seven unities of 4:4-6.
   All the divisions of the religious world — Christian, professed Christian, and non-Christian — are a result of violation of one or more of these seven unities. Instead of preserving the *one body,* men have created a multitude of denominations. Instead of clinging to the *one hope,* many have set their hope upon this world only. The "social gospel" places most of its hope upon making this sin-cursed world perfect.

2. The plea for *one body* is not a plea for denominational union or federation, since there were no denominations in Paul's time.

3. The *one body* is the church of Christ (Ephesians 1:22-23; Colossians 3:15; I Corinthians 12:13). Christ has only one

111

church. We can all be one body if we will accept and abide by God's Word as our only authority, and if we will receive and recognize as brothers all who are truly saved, and if membership in any one church (assembly or congregation) is recognized as sufficient qualification for membership in any other congregation.

4. The *one Spirit* is the Holy Spirit.

5. The *one hope* of the Christian has always rested upon the return of Christ and the blessings of the future life (Titus 2:13; I Peter 1:13). "Set your hope perfectly on the grace that is to be brought unto you at the revelation of Jesus Christ." "If in this life only we have hope in Christ, we are of all men most miserable" (I Corinthians 15:19). The corruption in the nature of sinners is not taken away by giving them sufficient food, clothing, shelter, and entertainment. The curse which God pronounced on the earth and man when Adam sinned (thorns, death, pain, labor, sweat, suffering, etc.) shall not be removed until the end of time (Revelation 22:3). The future does not look good, according to God's Word (II Timothy 3:1-6; II Peter 3:3; Matthew 24:37-39). Social progress is pleasant and desirable, but social progress has not kept our crime rate from climbing, nor will it ever make this world a paradise.

Fact Questions

187. What relationship does the "unity of the Spirit" have to the seven *ones* of 4:4-6?

188. What does the *one hope* of the Christian rest upon?

Text (4:5, 6)

5 one Lord, one faith, one baptism, 6 one God and Father of all, who is over all, and through all, and in all.

Thought Questions (4:5-6)

192. Did Paul have the question of sprinkling, pouring, or immersion in mind when he said, "There is one baptism"?

193. Is it correct to speak of "interfaith" activities? Why or why not?

194. Why should the fact that there is only one God make us to be united as Christians?

195. How can God be the "Father of all" when multitudes are "the children of the Devil"?

Paraphrase

5. The unity of the Spirit further consists of these unities: (4) the one Lord, Jesus Christ; (5) one faith, the Gospel; and (6) one baptism, immersion in water in the name of the Lord Jesus, that baptism which is the common experience of all the church.

6. And the grand apex of the seven unities that together make up the unity of the Spirit is the truth that (7) there is one God and Father of all, who is high above all things, but yet through all, and in all things. We must therefore be united, for we are all of one family, all brothers, children of one father.

Notes (4:5-6)

1. The one Lord is Jesus Christ. "He is Lord of all." (Compare Acts 10:36; 2:38; Romans 10:12; Matthew 28:18.) No pope, prophet, teacher, editor, elder, preacher, reformer, president, or any other man has authority to act as Lord of the church.

2. The *one faith* does not refer to the act of believing, but to the body of doctrines which we believe. The one faith is the Gospel. Philippians 1:27 speaks of those who were "striving together for THE FAITH of the gospel." See also Jude 3. It is not scriptural to speak of "many faiths" or "interfaith activities," as many do.

3. When speaking of the *one baptism*, Paul could not have had in mind the question of pouring, or sprinkling, or immersion. Only immersion was practiced in the time of the apostles. The earliest case of sprinkling for baptism on record is that of Novation in 251 A.D., who was "baptized" upon his bed while sick by pouring a large quantity of water over him. According to the historians, immersion was nearly the universal practice until the Middle Ages when the Roman Catholic church declared at the Council of Constance that immersion and sprinkling were of equal validity.

4. Paul was certainly not referring to Holy Spirit baptism as the *one baptism* that was the common experience of the church. Baptism in the Holy Spirit was a most exceptional experience. On the day of Pentecost the apostles were baptized in the Holy Spirit (Acts 1:5; 2:4). About ten years later, at the house of Cornelius, Peter saw the Holy Spirit fall on Cornelius and his household. In telling about

113

this, Peter said that the Holy Spirit fell on them, "as on us at the beginning. Then remembered I the word of the Lord how that he had said, John indeed baptized with water, but ye shall be baptized with the Holy Spirit" (Acts 11:15-16). These are the only cases of Holy Spirit baptism recorded in the Bible. The experiences of those who claim to have received the baptism in the Holy Spirit in modern times are so contradictory that no confidence can be placed in them.

5. If there is only one baptism, surely there ought not be any disagreement as to how it is to be performed, or in what it is done.

6. The Christian believes as firmly as does the Jew or Mohammedan that there is ONE God. However, the Christian accepts the profound revelation which God has given about Himself, namely that although He is one God, yet there are three perfectly harmonious identities within that one God: the Father, the Lord Jesus Christ, and the Holy Spirit.

7. God is called the "Father of all" in verse six, because He is the Father of all by creation. Of course, He is not the spiritual Father of sinners, and they cannot claim His blessings (John 8:44).

8. God is over all. He is supreme, high above all material and sinful things. God says, "I dwell in the high and holy place" (Isaiah 57:15).

9. God is through all. He is so omnipotent and powerful that He can do all things. No barriers limit His power.

10. God is in all. His power energizes the atom of all creation. He dwells not only in the high and holy place, but also with him that is of a contrite and humble spirit (Isaiah 57:15).

11. Since there is only one body, spirit, etc., Christians ought to be knit together as one. Being united by God upon these seven things is such a solid basis for unity that it ought to hold Christians together in spite of everything that tends to divide them.

Fact Questions

189. Who is the *one Lord*?
190. What is the *one faith*?
191. Why cannot the *one baptism* be Holy Spirit baptism?
192. Why cannot the teaching of *one baptism* have had reference to the question of sprinkling, pouring, or immersion?
193. In what three relationships does God stand to all things?
194. Quote Ephesians 4:4-6 from memory.

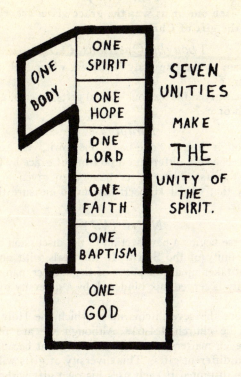

ONE BODY
ONE SPIRIT
ONE HOPE
ONE LORD
ONE FAITH
ONE BAPTISM
ONE GOD

SEVEN UNITIES MAKE **THE** UNITY OF THE SPIRIT.

GOD IS

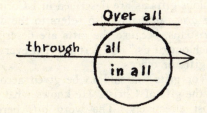

Over all

through all

in all

Text (4:7)

7 But unto each one of us was the grace given according to the measure of the gift of Christ.

Thought Questions (4:7)

196. How can we be one body in Christ when each of us is so different?
197. Who has given the various special gifts, talents, and abilities to each of us?

Paraphrase

7. But, though there is "one body, one spirit," etc., each one of us has received a different outpouring of grace by being given different gifts. These gifts have been given according to the way that Christ Himself saw fit to measure them out to each one.

Notes (4:7)

1. This verse begins a new section in the discussion about keeping the unity of the Spirit. It still deals with unity (see v. 13), but takes up a new phase of the subject, namely the fact that unity is served, not hindered, by a diversity of individual gifts.

2. There are the seven items upon which the Holy Spirit has united the church 4:4-6). Although we are united upon these seven matters, each of us is different because we have received different gifts. This diversity of gifts will not cause us to be disunited if each uses his own gift without envying others. Actually the difference in gifts helps, not hinders, in the work of perfecting the saints and building up the church.

3. The *grace* mentioned in this verse refers to particular gifts and abilities which Christ has given. Probably the primary reference is to the offices mentioned in Ephesians 4:12, and such miraculous gifts as are described in I Corinthians 12:8-10. But the *grace* probably also refers to the different abilities of Christians, because the gifts are described as being given to "each one of us," and certainly not everyone received miraculous gifts or offices.

4. The *grace* (or gifts) is said to be given according to the measure of the gift of Christ. He knows what gifts we can use the most effectively. The word *gift* here signifies a gratuity or expression of favor. Christ always gives bountifully and graciously.

The *gift of Christ* does not here refer to God's gift of His Son for us (John 3:16), but to Christ's own gracious bestowal of gifts to us. This is indicated by the next verse, 4:8.

5. Inasmuch as the gifts bestowed upon us come from Christ and the Holy Spirit, we should therefore find no harmful overlapping, no insufficiency in any necessary works, and no contradictions, for the Holy Spirit is never at odds with Himself.

Fact Questions

195. What does the word *grace* refer to in 4:7?
196. What effect does the fact that Christians have received differing gifts have upon their unity?
197. According to what measure has grace been dispensed to each one?

Text (4:8)

8 Wherefore he saith, when he ascended on high, he led captivity captive, and gave gifts unto men.

Thought Questions (4:8)

198. Who is it that has ascended on high?
199. What is the captivity which was taken captive? Can you think of anything (or any things) which holds men captive?
200. What gifts did Christ give to men after He ascended?

Paraphrase

8. As a proof that Christ has given different gifts to each one, note that the Scripture saith (Psalm 68:18), in referring to Christ, that when he ascended into the heights of heaven, he took captive the things that held man in captivity, and he gave gifts unto men.

Notes (4:8)

1. "Wherefore he saith" is more clearly translated, "Wherefore, it says," in Psalm 68:18, etc. Paul quoted this verse, which was actually a prophecy, to prove that Christ indeed had given various gifts to the members of the church.

2. Psalm 68, which is quoted here, is a psalm glorifying God for His power and victories in battle, for His wonders at Sinai and in the wilderness, and for His glory in the temple. Paul, by inspiration of God, informs us that at least part of the psalm had reference to our God and Savior, Jesus Christ.* Paul gives his interpretation of the passage in verse nine.

117

3. What is the _captivity_ which Christ led captive?

Some have thought that this is a reference to what Christ supposedly did after He died. This doctrine sets forth the idea that between the time of His death and resurrection Christ descended into Hades to preach, and to bring out the souls of the saints of Old Testament times. These saints supposedly could not previously be taken into God's presence because no atonement price had been paid for their sins before Christ died. It is our firm belief that this doctrine is not taught in the Bible, and contradicts many plain Bible teachings. See Appendix Art. I.

What, then, is the captivity which is referred to?

(1) _Sin_ — "Whosoever committeth sin is the servant (_doulos,_ slave) of sin" (John 8:34; Luke 4:18).

(2) _Fear of death_ — Christ died to "deliver them, who through fear of death, were all their lifetime subject to bondage" (Hebrews 2:15).

(3) _The law of sin_ — Romans 8:2-3. Our human weakness toward sin, and fleshly inclination toward sin is a great captivity from which Christ has granted us deliverance if we will receive it.

By His death and ascension, Christ has taken captive these things that formerly held His people captive, and in the time to come, He shall even redeem us from the captivity of death.

4. What gifts did Christ give unto men after He ascended? Victorious generals often gave to their warriors gifts from the spoils of battle, or from the royal treasure.

The gifts which Christ gave are listed in part in 4:11. These consisted of certain offices — apostles, prophets, evangelists, pastors, and teachers. Also the Holy Spirit is spoken of as a _gift,_ and the Holy Spirit was poured out after Christ ascended (Acts 2:33, 38; 11:15, 17).

*The INTERPRETER'S BIBLE says that as the rabbis had applied Psalm 68:18 to Moses going up onto Sinai, likewise the writer of Ephesians adopts a form of the text then current among the rabbis, and then follows it with an arbitrary _midrashic_ interpretation by applying it to Christ's ascension. Actually there is no more natural and obvious application of Psalm 68:18 possible than to apply it to Christ and His ascension. And since Paul, an inspired man, says that that is the meaning of it, all gainsaying should end.

5. Paul has been accused of misapplying Psalm 68:18 in this verse. He has been accused of using a form of the text which was different from the Hebrew version of Psalm 68:18. There is an *apparent* difference. In the psalm the text reads, "Thou hast *received* gifts for men." (Revised Version, "among men.") As quoted in Ephesians 4:8, it reads, that He *"gave* gifts unto men." There is actually no contradiction here between "receiving" (in Psalms) and "giving" (in Ephesians). The Hebrew word *lagach,* which ordinarily means to *take* or *receive,* sometimes carries the idea of taking something *for* someone else, which amounts to the same thing as giving it to them.

For example, Genesis 38:6: "And Judah took a wife for (gave one unto) Er, his firstborn." Paul has not misapplied the Old Testament Scriptures.

Fact Questions

198. Why did Paul quote Psalm 68:18?
199. What three things are listed as being part of the captivity which Christ led captive?
200. When did Christ give gifts to men?

Text (4:9, 10)

9 Now this, he ascended, what is it but that he also descended into the lower parts of the earth? 10 He that descended is the same also that ascended far above all the heavens, that he might fill all things.

Thought Questions (4:9-19)

201. If the Scripture speaks about God ascending, does not that imply that He must first have descended?
202. What are the *lower parts of the earth* into which Christ descended? Do you know what the phrase, *the lower parts of the earth,* is applied to in the Bible?
203. For what purpose did Christ descend and then ascend, according to verse ten?

Paraphrase

9. Now this statement in Psalm 68 that "He ascended," what can that imply, except that God, about Whom the Psalm is written, must have first descended into the earth, thus entering the "lower parts"? For God could not be said to have

119

ascended from heaven. He must needs have descended first
to the earth.

10. Since only Jesus Christ has descended, He is the one of
whom the Psalm speaks. He has descended, and He has
ascended far above all the heavens, that He might fill and
rule all things.

Notes (4:9-10)

1. These two verses are a parenthesis between verses eight and
eleven, to prove that the verse quoted from Psalm 68 can
apply only to Christ. Jesus Himself said in John 3:13, "No
man hath ascended up to heaven, but he that came down from
heaven, even the Son of man." This being true, when Psalm
68 spoke of one ascending into heaven, it must of necessity
have referred to Jesus, for He alone has descended from
heaven.

2. The *lower parts of the earth* into which Christ descended
refer to all the places into which Christ entered from His
conception in Mary, until His ascension.

   a. The *lower parts of the earth* may refer to the womb of
Mary, for David, in Psalm 139:13, 15 used the phrase
"lower parts of the earth" to refer to his mother's womb.

   b. The earth itself is the *lower parts* of the universe. Some
have taken the words, *the earth,* as being in apposition and
synonymous with the *lower parts.* For example, in the
phrase, *the city of Ephesus,* the city and Ephesus are the
same. Likewise, the *lower parts* and the *earth* may be
the same. (We mention this interpretation because it is
frequently suggested. Frankly, it seems a bit forced to us,
because it is hard to use a word in apposition to a com-
parative form like *the lower parts.*)

   c. The *lower parts of the earth* refer to the grave, and perhaps to Sheol (Hades), which is described as being an
underworld (Isaiah 14:9; Ezekiel 26:20). Note Psalm
63:9 "Those who seek my soul to destroy it shall go
into the lower parts of the earth."

     Christ certainly descended into the grave and into
Hades. Acts 2:27. Thus He was in the *lower parts of
the earth.*

     The tomb of Jesus is referred to as *the heart of the
earth* in Matthew 12:40: "For as Jonah was three days
and three nights in the whale's belly; so shall the Son

120

of man be three days and three nights in the heart of the earth."

3. Christ ascended "far above all the heavens." There are several heavens mentioned in the Scriptures. The *third heaven* is mentioned in II Corinthians 12:2. The atmosphere is spoken of as a *heaven* in such phrases as "the birds of heaven." Outer space is spoken of as a *heaven* in such phrases as "the stars of heaven" (Jeremiah 4:25; Deuteronomy 28:62). The Jewish rabbis spoke of seven *heavens*. Christ is so exalted that He is far above all the heavens. (Compare Hebrews 7:26.)

4. After Christ ascended, there was given unto Him dominion, glory, and a kingdom (Daniel 7:14). Truly, He fills all things, for in Him all things consist (or hold together). (See Colossians 1:17.)

Fact Questions

201. What is implied in the statement, *He ascended?*
202. What are the *lower parts of the earth* into which Christ descended?
203. How high did Christ ascend?
204. For what purpose did Christ ascend?

11 And he gave some to be apostles; and some prophets; and some evangelists; and some, pastors and teachers

Text (4:11)

Thought Questions (4:11)

204. How could the offices in the church be considered *gifts?*
205. Does the church of today have apostles?
206. What is the difference between an evangelist and a pastor?

Paraphrase

11. When Christ ascended on high, he gave gifts to men. These gifts consisted of certain offices and powers, such as apostles, and prophets, and evangelists, pastors and teachers.

Notes (4:11)

1. Servants of the gospel may take considerable pleasure in the thought that the various offices of the church are Christ's choice gifts to mankind.

The list of offices in this verse is not exhaustive. For a similar list of gifts, see I Corinthians 12:28.

2. The apostles were the special messengers, the eyewitnesses of Christ's resurrection (Acts 1:21-22; Luke 6:13). Men may still be called *apostles,* in the sense that anyone who is sent is an *apostle* of the one who sends him. But strictly speaking, the twelve apostles had no successors.

While the office of apostle was temporary, the teachings of the twelve apostles will always direct the church. In one sense, we can say that the church still has apostles, the same ones it had in the beginning.

3. The prophets held another temporary office. (See Zechariah 13:1-3; I Corinthians 13:8, see notes on 3:5 concerning the prophets.)

4. Preachers such as Timothy, Philip, etc., were called Evangelists (II Timothy 4:5; Acts 21:8). The word *evangelist* means a bringer of good news. Evangelists may be called *ministers* (I Timothy 4:6). This office, by its very nature, must be permanent in the church. Evangelists will be needed as long as any person on earth has not heard the good news.

5. The pastors and teachers are those who are elsewhere called *elders* (presbyters) or bishops (overseers) (Acts 20:17; Titus 1:5-7). These men are the overseers and teachers of individual congregations, and there should be more than one such *pastor* in each church (Acts 14:23).

The absence of the article *the* before *teachers* in the Greek text, plus the fact that it is connected with *pastors* by a different conjunction than is used to separate the other offices, seems to indicate that the *pastors and teachers* are the same office viewed from two different aspects, namely from the teaching and shepherding aspects.

The common notion that an evangelist is a travelling preacher who holds revivals, and a pastor is a located preacher, has no foundation in the Scripture. Any preacher or minister of the gospel may be called an *evangelist,* and the elders ought to be called *pastors.*

Pastors and teachers are, of course, permanent officers in the church.

6. The offices (or *gifts*) here listed were originally given by miraculous endowment. Even the offices that would remain permanently in the church were given miraculous help in the early years of the church. Evangelists were enabled to preach without long years of study and training. Pastors and teachers were empowered to do their work without the neces-

sity of long preparation. Such assistance was necessary to get the church firmly and quickly established, but there is no indication that such help was to be continued indefinitely.

Fact Questions

205. Name the five offices which Christ gave to be in the church at the beginning.
206. Which of the offices were permanent, and which were temporary?
207. Which two of the five offices probably refer to the same office under different names?
208. In what way were even the permanent offices miraculously given?

Text (4:12)

12 for the perfecting of the saints, unto the work of ministering, unto the building up of the body of Christ

Thought Questions (4:12)

207. What was it that was given for the perfecting of the saints, and the building up of the body of Christ? (See 4:11.)
208. Why do the saints need to be perfected?
209. When Christians are perfected, what work should they do?

Paraphrase

12. The different gifts that Christ gave to the church — apostles, prophets, etc. — were given to bring about the perfecting of the saints, who are then to devote themselves unto the work of ministering. This perfecting of the saints and their work of ministering will lead unto the growth and building up of the church, the body of Christ.

Notes (4:12)

1. *Perfecting* means "equipping, fitting out, preparing, or strengthening." Every new Christian needs to be fitted out for service to Christ. Especially was this true of the Christians of the apostolic age, most of whom had been idolaters and knew little about the true God and His ways.
2. When saints are perfected, they are to devote themselves to the work of ministering, such as ministering to the needs of the afflicted and the untaught. Every Christian household should imitate the example of the house of Stephanas, who

addicted themselves to the ministry of the saints (I Corinthians 16:15). That would be a wonderful type of addiction: We have perverted the scriptural concept of the word *ministering,* until it has become in most people's minds a description of a "clergyman's" work. ALL of us are to devote ourselves to ministering, which includes helping both the material and spiritual needs of people.

3. When the officers which Christ has *given* for the church are doing their work, and getting the people to do their work, then the churches will be building up. They will be growing in numbers, piety, good works, and happiness.

Fact Questions

209. For what purpose were the gifts given?
210. When the saints are perfected, what work will they do?
211. Unto what will the perfecting and ministering of the saints lead?

Text (4:13)

13 till we all attain unto the unity of the faith, and of the knowledge of the Son of God, unto a fullgrown man, unto the measure of the stature of the fulness of Christ:

Thought Questions (4:13)

210. What is it that was to last "till we all attain unto the unity of the faith"? (Verses 11 and 12 can help you answer this.)
211. When did, or when will, "we all attain unto the unity of the faith"?
212. By what means should the church be able to come to a unity of the knowledge of the Son of God?
213. Is the *fullgrown man* a description of what we are to become as individuals, or a description of the whole church when it is fully matured?
214. Unto what measure are we to grow? Is it actually possible to attain unto this measure?

Paraphrase

13. The gifts which Christ gave to the church for its building up are to continue until we all attain unto the unity of the faith, and the unity of the knowledge of Christ the Son of God; unto a state of development when we shall be like a fullgrown man; and indeed develop unto that required meas-

124

ure of growth wherein we shall have reached the stature of the fullness of Christ.

Notes (4:13)

1. According to 4:3, we already have a unity which needs only to be kept or guarded. Here we are told that we must *attain unto unity.* We may be only one body in the sight of God, but this oneness is often strained to the breaking point. Even in Paul's time the Jewish and Gentile Christians had little unity. They would probably have had no unity at all if Paul and others had not labored as they did. The Word of God was not yet fully revealed at that time. Hence, there were many things that we know and can be united upon which were at that time matters of uncertainty.

2. The phrase, *unity of the faith,* probably means the unity demanded by faith in Christ. Our differing gifts and backgrounds should not keep us from having unity. In fact, the differences among us only serve to meet many needs. No one member can do everything necessary. Every member depends on every other member to do those things that he cannot do. Therefore, our differences should help us to attain unity, rather than hinder it.

3. We are also to attain to the unity of the *knowledge of Christ.* The knowledge mentioned here is precise, personal knowledge of Christ, not merely a knowledge of who He is, but a close personal acquaintance and a profound understanding of Him. The church should have been able to attain unto such knowledge when the apostles had finished their teachings and writings.

4. Verse 4:13 seems to set a time limit on the gifts of Christ. They were to last "till we all attain to the unity of the faith." It might seem that the church has never yet attained to the unity of the faith. However, this goal was almost a reality in the latter part of the first century. The church then reached a degree of unity of belief, fellowship, and practice that it has not duplicated since that time.

In the early generations after the church was established, Christ gave it many gifts and powers to hasten its growth from infancy to a fullgrown man. (See I Corinthians 12:8-11 and Ephesians 4:11 for lists of such gifts.)

While these gifts may have sometimes been given directly from Christ, we know that they were given by the laying on

125

of the apostles' hands. However, those upon whom the apostles laid their hands apparently could not pass on the gifts that they received (II Timothy 1:6; Romans 1:11; Acts 8:17, 18).

At that time, the New Testament was not completed, as we have it today. Not all of the New Testament books had been written, nor were those which were written collected together into one group and widely distributed. If a man wished to preach the gospel, he had no book of authority and information to rely upon as we have. To take care of this temporary deficiency, Christ bestowed various gifts upon the church.

For example: A man who received the gift of *knowledge* or *prophecy* could know and preach the gospel without having to spend years in study and preparation. WE, however, are told to study in order to show ourselves approved unto God (II Timothy 2:15). A person with the gift of *tongues,* or *interpretation of tongues,* could go into a foreign area and speak so as to be understood without the struggle of having to learn a new language. The power to do this would be a mighty sign to unbelievers. A person with the gift of *discerning of spirits* could detect false teaching without having a Bible to prove that the teacher was a deceiver.

By these gifts, Christ enabled the church to become quickly rooted and to spread rapidly. It was very important in that early age that the gospel should quickly and securely take root all over the world.

But the gifts actually belonged to the "childish" age of the church. Paul tells us in I Corinthians 13:8-11 that the spiritual gifts were like *childish things*. When the church became a fullgrown man, it would put away childish things, such as prophecies, tongues, knowledge.

In accordance with this, we find that the spiritual gifts that existed in the early generations of the church began to disappear after the lifetime of the apostles.

While many people have claimed to have supernatural gifts even down to the present time, we do not find people on earth today who can work miracles like Christ and His apostles did. We are of the persuasion that the gifts were only to last "till we all attain unto the unity of the faith," and we understand that this took place when the writings of the apostles were completed and made available to the church.

Of course, the permanent officers which Christ gave to the church are still with us. They serve as God's appointed agents to lead the church once again to the unity of the faith.

5. The church is described as the *body of Christ* in many places in Ephesians. It is therefore most appropriate to describe the fully matured church as a *fullgrown man.*

6. Ephesians 4:13 discusses the church as a whole, rather than as individual members. It is "we *all*" who are to come into the unity of the faith and of the knowledge of the Son of God, unto a fullgrown man.

7. As stated in the notes on Ephesians 1:23, the term *fulness* has a passive sense: "that which is filled." If we are to develop spiritually until we measure up to the stature of that which is filled by Christ, we ought to develop very greatly, and arrive at a time of life when we shall be like Christ Who has filled us.

Fact Questions

212. What was to last until the church attained unto the unity of the faith?
213. What are the three things listed in Ephesians 4:13 that the church was to attain unto?
214. According to the notes, when did the church attain unto the unity of the faith, etc.?

Text (4:14)

14 that we may be no longer children, tossed to and fro and carried about with every wind of doctrine, by the sleight of men, in craftiness, after the wiles of error;

Thought Questions (4:14)

215. How is a young Christian who is exposed to many conflicting teachings like a ship on a stormy sea?
216. Why are the young easily led to accept falsehoods?
217. Are false teachers always bad, working by the "sleight of men, in craftiness"? Are not some of them sincere?
218. What are *wiles?* Why does error use wiles?

Paraphrase

14. The church must develop into a fullgrown man, so that we may no longer be children in spiritual development. Spiritual

127

children are like ships on a stormy sea, tossed about and carried around by every wind of teaching they hear. And those teachings which toss the uninstructed to and fro are often most deceptive, being presented by the dishonest methods of men, and by every cunning way of working that is suited to the wiles of error.

Notes (4:14)

1. The word *children* used here refers to little children or infants, those who are young Christians. Such little children will believe almost anything that they may be told, even if it is a lie. We should not long remain in spiritual infancy, and there is no need of so remaining.

2. The force of false doctrine upon the uninstructed is like the force of a storm upon a ship without a rudder.

3. The winds of doctrine that blow the uninstructed around "blow" in (or by) two things:
   (1) In the sleight of men.
   (2) In craftiness after the wiles of error. (Rotherham translates this: "In knavery suited to the artifice of error.")

4. The word *sleight* (from *Kubos*, meaning cube) actually refers to dice-playing. The false doctrines that are taught are sometimes presented by dishonest means, even as dice players use dishonesty. Like a small child who finds himself the victim of card sharks, so is an untrained soul before the winds of doctrine.

5. The term *craftiness* carries the idea of bad working. The root of the word means "all workings." False teachers do not overlook a single opportunity to promote their doctrines.

   This craftiness is practiced by the wiles (or trickeries) of error. Wiles are tricks, or sneaky schemes. Error never comes out into the open and honestly represents itself. It uses wiles to deceive the unsuspecting. (Compare Ephesians 6:11.)

6. Error is never harmless, nor are false teachers good. They may be morally outstanding, like wolves in sheep's clothing. In fact, they may not even be aware of their own errors. But this does not make them harmless. In truth, those who live good and exemplary lives but do not teach the truth are the most dangerous people of all.

Fact Questions

215. What are we no longer to be (4:14)?
216. What is it that tosses and blows about those who are spiritual children?
217. In (or by) what two things do the *winds of doctrine* blow?
218. To what does the word *sleight* refer? What does this indicate about those who teach false doctrines?

Text (4:15)

15 but speaking truth in love, may grow up in all things into him, who is the head, *even* Christ;

Thought Questions (4:15)

219. Why must truth be spoken in love? Can truth be spoken without love? Can love be demonstrated without speaking the truth?
220. Is there any difference between becoming like Christ and "growing up into Christ"?

Paraphrase

15. Rather than remaining spiritual children who are subject to such perils, we must grow up. As we grow, we must live according to truth in everything we do. Then we shall grow up in all things into Christ, who is the head of the church.

Notes (4:15)

1. Verse fourteen told us what we should not do: "Be no more children." This verse tells us what we should do: "Grow up into Christ."

   We should not merely imitate some of Christ's good characteristics. We must grow up *INTO* Him. Our nature, thoughts, and deeds should be absorbed into those of Christ. As we serve Him, pray unto Him, and learn of Him, we shall grow into Him.

2. *Speaking truth* carries the idea of living the truth, or of "truthing it," or "pursuing truth" (Rotherham). It is very hard to be completely truthful at all times, but such is the will of God for us.

3. Truth and love must be joined together. Together they are powerful. Truth can be uttered without love. We can have such a superior attitude that the truth we speak will repel people instead of attracting them.

129

However, you cannot show real love without holding to the truth. It is not true love to allow a person to go to hell to avoid hurting his feelings. "By this we know that we love the children of God, when we love God, and keep his commandments. For this is the love of God that we keep his commandments" (I John 5:2-3).

4. The New Testament repeatedly emphasizes that Christ is the head of the church.

Fact Questions

219. How must we speak truth?
220. Into Whom are we to grow?
221. In what things are we to grow up into Christ?

Text (4:16)

16 from whom all the body fitly framed and knit together through that which every joint supplieth, according to the working in *due* measure of each several part, maketh the increase of the body unto the building up of itself in love.

Thought Questions (4:16)

221. Who is it "from whom all the body (is) fitly framed"?
222. Can you find the principal parts (subject, predicate, and object) of verse sixteen?
223. This verse says that the body (the church) must be fitly framed and *knit* together. What does the word *knit* mean when applied to the human body, as to a broken bone, for example? How would this indicate that the members of the church should be joined together?
224. What must each several part do if the body is to make increase?
225. What is that which "every joint supplieth" that causes the body to be knit together and to make increase?
226. When does the church build itself up in love?

Paraphrase

16. From Christ, the head, all the body is bound together closely, indeed even coalesced or grown together. This joining is done as that vital supply of spiritual life passes from Christ through every joint (contact) to the parts next to it. And when every single member of the body is thus functioning in the measure that it should, the whole body will make the increase of the body, and it will build itself up in love.

Notes (4:16)

1. Stripped of its many qualifying phrases, the gist of verse sixteen is this: "The whole body — makes the increase of the body." In other words, all the members of the church must work together if the church is going to grow.

    The evil in the church today is that we lay too much stress on certain offices and too little on the work required of every member of the body.

2. *Fitly framed* means "bound together, joined together closely." As bones are bound together at the joints by ligaments, so all members of the body of Christ are closely joined together.

    Knit together suggests "growing together, or coalesced." The members of the church are not just placed side by side, but should become coalesced into one living body. The ties that bind brethren in Christ are as close as those that bind the leg bone to the thigh bone.

3. *Through that which every joint supplieth* literally reads, "through every joint of the supply."

    Christ, of course, furnishes the *supply*, the vital nourishment of the spiritual body. This vital supply goes out from Christ through every joint of the body to the parts next to it. Thus the members are knit together.

    This suggests that as we have been nourished in spiritual things from Christ, we must pass on our spiritual sustenance to the members of the body next to us. Thus the whole body will be knit together.

4. Each member of the body (church) must function according to the working in due measure of each single part. When one part of the human body fails to function, the whole body suffers. The same thing happens in the church.

5. The church builds itself up in love when every member is working to make the increase of the body. A church that is busy, and has its members working to win souls, usually has no time for quarreling. It builds itself up in love.

Fact Questions

222. What is the gist of Ephesians 4:16, stripped of its many qualifying phrases?
223. What is supplied from Christ? Through what does it pass?
224. How must each several part of the body work?
225. In what does the body build itself up when it is increasing?

EPHESIANS 4:16

EVERY MEMBER MUST WORK

IF THE CHURCH IS TO INCREASE

IF THE CHURCH

FROM CHRIST (The Head)

ALL THE BODY

JOINED TOGETHER HARMONIOUSLY

AND KNIT TOGETHER INTO

ONE ORGANISM

This knitting is done by that

which every joint supplies to

the part next to it.

Each member working in the

measure that is due

MAKES THE INCREASE

OF THE BODY.

Previewing in Outline Form (4:17-5:2)

B. Walk as becometh saints. 4:17-5:20.
    1. Walk not as the Gentiles walk. 4:17-24.
        a. The command. 4:17a.
        b. The Gentile walk. 4:17b-19.
            (1) In the vanity of their mind. 4:17b.
            (2) Darkened in understanding. 4:18a.
            (3) Alienated from the life of God. 4:18b.
                (a) Because of the ignorance in them.
                (b) Because of the hardening of their heart.
            (4) Given over to lasciviousness. 4:19.
                (a) Because they were past feeling.
                (b) To work all uncleanness with greediness.
        c. The Christian's walk. 4:20-24.
            (1) Different from the Gentile's walk. 4:20-21.
            (2) Must put away our former manner of life. 4:22.
            (3) Must be renewed in the spirit of your mind. 4:23.
            (4) Must put on the new man. 4:24.
    2. Seven practical exhortations. 4:25-5:2.
        a. Speak the truth. 4:25.
        b. Control your anger. 4:26-27.
        c. Steal no more. 4:28.
        d. Speak that which is good. 4:29.
        e. Grieve not the Holy Spirit. 4:30.
        f. Put away angry talk and attitudes. 4:31.
        g. Be imitators of God. 4:32-5:2.
            (1) Be kind.
            (2) Be tenderhearted.
            (3) Be forgiving.
            (4) Walk in love. 5:2.

Text (4:17-19)

17 This I say therefore, and testify in the Lord, that ye no longer walk as the Gentiles also walk, in the vanity of their mind, 18 being darkened in their understanding, alienated from the life of God, because of the ignorance that is in them, because of the hardening of their hearts; 19 who being past feeling gave themselves up to lasciviousness, to work all uncleanness with greediness.

Thought Questions (4:17-19)

227. Was it a simple task for the Ephesian Christians to *walk no longer as the Gentiles walk?*

228. Paul seems to condemn the Gentiles quite heavily. Did the Gentiles as a whole live baser lives than the Jews?

229. Did Paul mean to imply by his use of the word *Gentile* that non-Christians should be called *Gentiles,* regardless of their race?

230. What is *vanity?* What Old Testament book exposes many things as being *vanity?*

231. Describe the condition of the Gentiles' understanding.

232. Are the Gentiles aware that they are alienated from the life of God? Is there any other source of life, except from God?

233. Note that the Gentiles are alienated from God because of the ignorance that is in them. What should this teach us about the state of the heathen who do not know God at present?

234. What happens to the conscience when we harden our hearts and do not do what we know we should?

235. Can a person get to the point that he is no longer pained by conscience?

236. To what type of conduct do people without feelings of guilt and shame always give themselves (v. 19)?

Paraphrase

17. Now this I say, and bear testimony with all the seriousness of one who knows the Lord and is serving Him, that you must no longer be walking, that is, living each day, as other Gentiles walk. For they live according to the useless and perverse disposition of their minds, and not according to what is good and of God.

18. The Gentiles are covered with darkness in their understanding. They are shut off from the life which God bestows, on account of the ignorance that is in them, and on account of the callusing of their hearts.

19. They have gone so far in sin that they have lost all feeling of guilt and pain of conscience when they do wrong. Having no restraints within them, they have given themselves over to unbridled lust and shamelessness, to work all manner of uncleanness with unrestrained desires to have more of forbidden pleasures.

Notes (4:17-19)

1. It took a lot of courage for the Ephesian Christians to *no longer walk as the Gentiles walk.* They lived in the shadow of the glorious temple of Diana, and with milling thousands of her worshippers. To refuse to associate in the practices of their former friends took much conviction and courage.

   It still takes a lot of courage to *walk no longer as the Gentiles walk.* Social drinking, lewd motion pictures, night clubs, dancing, card-playing, and many other things that are displeasing to God are so much a part of modern American life that many Christians compromise their standards. Let us resolutely refuse to walk any longer as the Gentiles walk.

2. Some modern commentaries make a great deal of the use of the word *Gentiles* in verse seventeen, attempting to prove that Paul could not have written Ephesians. It is alleged that *Gentiles* is contrasted with *Christians,* and that Paul never conceived of such a contrast as church members being *Israelites, and* non-Christians being *Gentiles.*

   It is by no means implied in this verse that all non-Christians are to be called *Gentiles.* The word *Gentiles* in the verse obviously refers to non-Christian Gentiles. There were far more Gentiles living in and around Ephesus than there were Jews. The Ephesian church was predominantly Gentile. Quite naturally, therefore, Paul would speak to the Ephesians about how the *Gentiles* lived when he wanted to make a contrast between the lives of the Christians and the lives of the non-Christians.

   The Gentiles around Ephesus were much given to magic, immorality, and high-mindedness before their conversion to Christ. Generally they lived much more sinful lives than the Jews. The Jews were not perfect, but they had known God and His Law for centuries, and did not walk in the idolatry and vain practices that were nearly universal among the Gentiles. Paul did not want his converts to continue to live as the Gentiles had always lived.

   However, even if Paul did use the word *Gentiles* to denote non-Christians, it would not be un-Pauline. For in Galatians 6:16 he speaks of the church as the *Israel of God.* (Compare also Romans 2:28-29; 9:6-8; Philippians 3:3.)

3. *Vanity* is that which is devoid of truth and appropriateness; that which is worthless, useless, and has no good about it. In the book of Ecclesiastes, King Solomon exposed many

things that the world thinks are excellent (such as laughter, lust, liquor, learning, real estate, riches) as "vanity, and a striving after wind." But the Gentiles (and also most unconverted Jews) are still striving after such things. Christians have been redeemed from their *vain* manner of life (I Peter 1:18).

4. The world considers itself too wise to believe the teachings of the Bible. Actually, this attitude is not due to wisdom, but to a darkening in its mind. Satan has blinded the minds of the unbelieving (II Corinthians 4:4).

5. God gives life to all. Hence, it is a perversion of nature to depart from the life of God. But the Gentiles are shut off from the life of God, being aliens to God's kingdom. (See the notes on 2:12, 19.) They are alienated for two reasons:
   (1) The ignorance that is in them.
   (2) The hardening (callusing) of their heart.
   Note that the Gentiles did not know much, and that God does not excuse ignorance. Furthermore, they hardened their hearts against that which they did know.

6. The King James Version wrongly has *blindness* for *hardening* in 4:18. The skin on the hands develops a hardening or callus when it is exposed to pressure and work. Likewise, when the conscience is rubbed hard and its guidance ignored, it develops a hardening or callus. However, instead of being a protection from injury, this is merely a dulling of our finest nature.

7. Sin is like anesthesia. At first, it is offensive, and our conscience revolts against it. However, if we do not get away from it, it soon becomes less offensive to us, and then finally overpowering. We could also compare it to the cold of the great North, which can benumb its victims until they are doomed, but feel no cold. Being *past feeling* is the last stage before destruction. If your conscience never bothers you any more, you are in terrible peril.

8. Those who lose all feeling of guilt go readily into lasciviousness. *Lasciviousness* is a term that includes adultery, fornication, immodesty, shameless dress and speech, indecent behavior, etc. All of these things are natural for one who has thrown aside the feelings of conscience. Nothing is more terrible than the loss of shame. Immodesty should embarrass or anger us. If it does not, we need only to remove the checks of circumstances to complete the descent into sin.

9. The Gentiles do not do iniquity hesitantly, but with greediness or eagerness. This term *greediness* (Authorized Version, *covetousness*) refers to a greedy desire to have more. They desire the pleasures of sin, and go greedily after them.

Fact Questions

226. How were the Ephesians forbidden to walk?
227. In what do most Gentiles walk (v. 17)?
228. What was the condition of the understanding of the Gentiles?
229. For what two reasons were the Gentiles alienated from the life of God?
230. To what did the Gentiles give themselves (v. 19)?

Text (4:20-22)

20 But ye did not so learn Christ; 21 if so be that ye heard him, and were taught in him, even as truth is in Jesus: 22 that ye put away, as concerning your former manner of life, the old man, that waxeth corrupt after the lusts of deceit;

Thought Questions (4:20-22)

237. Can one be taught of Christ so as not to be taught as the truth is in Jesus?
238. If we have heard of Christ according to truth, what are we to put away?
239. Are we Christians in truth because we know and accept correct words and doctrines (v. 22)?
240. Is *putting away* our old man to be done once for all, or is it a gradual process?
241. Do sinners get better with age and experience? What does it mean when it says the "old man waxeth corrupt"?
242. What are *lusts of deceit?* What is deceitful about lusts?

Paraphrase

20. You Ephesians who learned the gospel did not learn of Christ to work uncleanness with greediness, so as to think these things allowable.
21. Assuming that you have heard of Christ and were taught according to what is truth in Jesus,
22. then ye were taught that you must put away all that concerns your manner of life before becoming a Christian; for that old man was getting worse and worse, decaying more and more, just as deceitful lusts always cause a spiritual decay.

Notes (4:20-22)

1. *Learn Christ* means more than to learn certain doctrines. True knowledge of Christ must produce a transformed life.

2. Truth in Jesus consists in putting away our former manner of life, and of putting on the new man, and of being renewed in the spirit of our mind. The Romish doctrine that a person can be morally bad and still be in good standing in the church is not of truth as it is in Jesus.

3. *Put away* and *put on* (4:22, 24) are verbs in the aorist imperative which indicates completed action, done one time. *Be renewed* (4:23) is in the present imperative, indicating continuous progressive action. This teaches us that repentance must be a thorough break with sin. There should be no gradual putting away the old man. However, the development of the new man is a progressive process.

4. *Lusts of deceit* are deceitful lusts. The things we desire (lust for) in this world promise thrills, and satisfaction. Instead they bring only disappointment, shame, disgrace, and contention.

5. Our old man, our former life before we accepted Christ, was becoming more and more corrupt through the deceitful desires he sought after. (See II Timothy 3:13.) Age and experience usually do not improve sinners. Their consciences become duller, and habits of evil more firmly fixed.

6. *Conversation* in the King James Version (v. 22) means our *manner of life*.

Fact Questions

231. If the Ephesians learned of Christ as truth is, what would they put away?

232. What is happening to the sinner's nature (the *old man*)?

Text (4:23, 24)

23 and that ye be renewed in the spirit of your mind, 24 and put on the new man, that after God hath been created in righteousness and holiness of truth.

Thought Questions (4:23, 24)

243. What is the spirit of our mind?

244. How can the spirit of our mind be renewed?

245. What is the *new man* which we are to put on?

246. After Whom have we been created? In what sense is the converted man *created?*

247. How does God create us *in righteousness?* Do we not perform our own righteousness?

248. What do you think the phrase *holiness of truth* means?

Paraphrase

23. You Ephesians must not only put off the old nature, but be renewing yourselves in the spirit that directs your mind.

24. Put on the new man, that new disposition and nature, which has been created in the likeness of God in righteousness and true holiness.

Notes (4:23, 24)

1. *Be renewed* is a continuous duty and process.

2. The *spirit of your mind* is the spirit that directs your mind. Before conversion it was a disobedient spirit. Now it must be a spirit of meekness, humility, and obedience.

3. How often in the Bible are righteousness and Christian character compared to garments which may be put on or off! Thus we note that Christians *can* improve themselves with God's help. We do not have to be the same old detestable persons always. We can put on a new man.

4. The new man, or new nature, is *created* (II Corinthians 5:17; Ephesians 2:10). The change in people that comes through faith and the incoming of the Holy Spirit is as great as the act that God wrought when He created the material universe. We are created after GOD. We are not created to be like the great men of this world, but to be like God (I John 3:1).

5. We are created *in righteousness,* because we have no righteousness in ourselves. Christ Jesus is our righteousness (I Corinthians 1:30). God takes away our sins when we are saved, and declares us righteous as a result of what He has done for us. Of course, after being thus created in righteousness, we must live soberly, righteously, and godly (Titus 2:12).

6. *Holiness of truth* means true holiness, not holiness which is just ceremonial or pretended. We were *created* to develop a Godlike character, true holiness. We are not saved merely to escape from hell and receive blessings.

Fact Questions

233. In what are we to be renewed?

234. What are we to put on?

235. After Whom are we created?

236. In what two ways are we created after God?

EPHESIANS 4:25 - 5:2

SEVEN PRACTICAL EXHORTATIONS

1. SPEAK THE TRUTH; 4:25

2. CONTROL YOUR ANGER; 4:26-27

3. STEAL NO MORE; 4:28

4. SPEAK THAT WHICH IS GOOD; 4:29

5. GRIEVE NOT THE HOLY SPIRIT; 4:30

6. PUT AWAY ANGRY TALK
   AND ATTITUDES; 4:31

7. BE IMITATORS OF GOD; 4:32-5:2
   -BE KIND
   -TENDERHEARTED
   -FORGIVING
   -WALK IN LOVE 5:2

Text (4:25-27)

25 Wherefore, putting away falsehood, speak ye truth each one with his neighbor: for we are members one of another. 26 Be ye angry and sin not: let not the sun go down upon your wrath: 27 neither give place to the devil.

Thought Questions (4:25-27)

249. What is the force of the *wherefore* in v. 25? Compare the preceding verses before you answer.
250. Why should the fact that we are members one of another curb our lying?
251. Did Paul command us to be angry? Harmonize 4:26 with 4:31.
252. Did Paul forbid us to be angry?
253. What is the danger in anger?
254. How long is wrath to be permitted to continue?
255. What does it mean when it says, "Neither give place to the devil"?
256. Is there any connection between being angry and giving place to the devil?

Paraphrase

25. Because you are new creatures in Christ, created by God in true holiness, you must observe such practical duties as to stop lying to one another, and to speak the truth to your neighbors. This we must do because we are members one of another in the church.
26. Furthermore, we must keep anger under control that we sin not. You may have anger arise at times, but let it not be prolonged. Put it away before the sun goes down.
27. Neither give an opportunity to the devil to control your actions, which can easily be done if anger is prolonged.

Notes (4:25-27)

1. After the lofty exhortations of 4:23-24, Paul brings us down to earth with a jolt in these verses. We have been created in righteousness and true holiness. *Wherefore,* on account of that, certain duties are laid upon us.
2. Verse 25 begins a series of seven practical exhortations concerning the walk of the Christian. See the outline.
3. The admonition to put away falsehood and speak the truth always is very hard to keep, but it is repeatedly commanded

141

in the New Testament. Verse 4:25 is a quotation from Zechariah 8:16.

4. In the church we are all members of Christ, and therefore members of one another. Now, in the human body, if one member, the nerves, were paralyzed, and lied to the stomach by carrying no sensations of hunger, the body might refuse all food and destroy itself. Likewise in the church, any lie by one member affects all the other members of the body. When one member is known to have lied, the whole church is discredited.

5. Verse 4:26 is a quotation of Psalm 4:4, where the reading is, "Stand in awe and sin not." (The Revised Version margin reads, "Be ye angry and sin not.") This is not a command to be angry but a caution not to sin when we are angry. People often do things when they are angry that they would not normally do.

While it is not a command to be angry, neither is it a prohibition of anger. Sometimes anger is necessary. Paul was occasionally angry (Acts 13:9-10; 23:3). Even Christ Jesus felt anger (Mark 3:5). We need to have convictions strong enough to have strong feelings about wickedness.

Nonetheless, while anger may sometimes be justified, it must be speedily cooled down. Anger should subside the same day it arises. When the sun has gone down, let anger be gone.

The anger upon which the sun is not to go down is anger that expresses itself in exasperation and wrath, the anger in which one is almost beside himself.

6. If anger is held very long, it becomes malice and hatred and resentment, and produces a desire for revenge. It gives a place (opportunity) to the devil to lead us into transgression and self-ruination.

7. While there is a connection between anger and giving place to the devil, there are also other ways we can give a place to the devil. For examples, (1) meditating upon lustful things, (2) meditating upon our unfair share of earthly riches, (3) reading books that undermine faith and morals.

Fact Questions

237. What is the reason we are to speak truth to our neighbors?
238. What are we to be careful not to do when angry?

239. How long is anger to be allowed to continue?
240. To whom are we not to give place?

Text (4:28)

28 Let him that stole steal no more: but rather let him labor, working with his hands the thing that is good, that he may have whereof to give to him that hath need.

Thought Questions (4:28)

257. Are there thieves in the church?
258. Can this verse be harmonized with the Communist doctrine of state ownership of all property?
259. What is the grand purpose of our labor?

Paraphrase

28. Let anyone in the church who is stealing steal no more. But rather let him toil, working with his own hands which were formerly used to steal, doing work which is good, so that he may have the means to maintain himself, and to share with those who have need.

Notes (4:28)

1. It may seem strange that Christians should have to be taught not to steal. But stealing is not uncommon. Nowadays there are many sophisticated forms of stealing — embezzlement, cheating on tax reports, driving hard bargains, misrepresenting goods, loafing on the employer's time, shortening an employee's time, cheating on examinations, etc. Let him that stole — regardless of how he did it, or what he stole — steal no more.

2. The best antidote for stealing is working. The word *labor* here implies wearisome, exhausting toil.

3. It is plainly taught here that work is not only for selfish gain, but to help others. Honesty is inculcated by an appeal to the highest motives. And this verse certainly does not teach us to steal from the rich to give to the poor. We must work if we want to have the means to help those in need.

4. This verse cannot be harmonized with Communist doctrine. The verse commands private generosity. But private ownership of property is a necessity if we are to have anything to give to others. Communism destroys private ownership, and makes all things state property.

143

Fact Questions

241. What is the one who steals to do?
242. With what is the ex-thief to work?
243. What type of work is the ex-thief to do?
244. What is the noble objective for which we toil and labor?

Text (4:29)

29 Let no corrupt speech proceed out of your mouth, but such as is good for edifying as the need may be, that it may give grace to them that hear.

Thought Questions (4:29)

260. How often is our conversation actually uttered with a purpose in mind of edifying and giving grace to those who hear us?
261. What types of utterance could be called *corrupt speech*?
262. How can speech give grace to them that hear?

Paraphrase

29. Let no rotten utterances go out from your mouth, but rather let that go out of your mouth which is good for building up people who may be in need of encouragement, correction, or instruction. Such speech will bring pleasure and profit to them that hear.

Notes (4:29)

1. Christians must carefully control their speech at all times. Do not let any speech that is rotten and corrupt go out of your mouth. (Compare Ephesians 5:4; Matthew 12:36-37.) Words are not simply so much wind. They carry with them the personality and thoughts of the speaker. As character can be rotten and produce evil, words can also be corrupt, for they reflect character.
2. Words are very powerful. They can fill many needs, such as giving instruction, encouragement, and correction.

Fact Questions

245. What type of speech is not to be let out of our mouths?
246. What type of speech is to be uttered?
247. What is our speech to give unto those that hear?

Text (4:30)

30 And grieve not the Holy Spirit of God, in whom ye were sealed unto the day of redemption.

144

Thought Questions (4:30)

263. If the Holy Spirit can be grieved, is the Holy Spirit a personality, or some impersonal influence?

264. How can we grieve the Holy Spirit?

265. Where does the Holy Spirit live (I Corinthians 6:19)?

Paraphrase

30. In all of life's activities, such as working, speaking, etc., be not grieving the Holy Spirit of God, that divine one in whom we are sealed and stamped as God's own until that day when our bodies are redeemed at the resurrection.

Notes (4:30)

1. We grieve the Holy Spirit by wicked actions and rotten speech. We grieve Him when we violate the commandments of the Spirit as given in Ephesians, chapter four. The Holy Spirit is sensitive. Holiness is always sensitive. Purity grows in sensitivity.

2. Israel grieved the Holy Spirit by their sins in the wilderness and in the land of Canaan (Isaiah 63:10).

3. How terrible it is to make the Holy Spirit which strengthens our inward man to be sorrowful and offended (Ephesians 3:16)!

4. See notes on Ephesians 1:13-14 for comments on being sealed with the Holy Spirit until the day of redemption.

Fact Questions

248. Whom are we not to grieve?

249. Unto what day are we sealed?

Text (4:31, 32)

31 Let all bitterness, and wrath, and anger, and clamor, and railing, be put away from you with all malice: 32 and be ye kind one to another, tenderhearted, forgiving each other, even as God also in Christ forgave you.

145

Thought Questions (4:31, 32)

266. Is a Christian's personality any concern to God?
267. Is it really possible to control feelings of bitterness, malice, etc.?
268. How should we forgive each other?

Paraphrase

31. In particular, grieve not the Holy Spirit by an evil disposition. Let all of the sharp, spiteful ways of feeling and speaking, along with anger, both in outbursts and temperament, and loud clamor, and blasphemous speech, be put away from you along with all ill will toward others. For these things displease the Spirit.

32. Having put away evil traits and dispositions, be kind one to another, tenderhearted, graciously forgiving each other, as also God in Christ has graciously forgiven you of even greater offences against Himself.

Notes (4:31, 32)

1. *Bitterness* is sharpness, harshness, spitefulness, resentment.
2. *Wrath* is anger erupting, anger that boils over but soon subsides.
3. *Anger* is a settled disposition of indignation, and angry outlook upon everything.
4. *Clamor* is a loud outcry, loud speech based on ungoverned feelings.
5. *Railing* is blasphemy, slander, speech injurious to another's good name, especially against God.
6. *Malice* is ill will, desire to injure.
7. These evils are common among many disciples of Christ, in spite of the fact that they are utterly contrary to our calling, contrary to the Father, and contrary to the Holy Spirit within us. They are old cruel hounds from past life, from

146

which we should have escaped long ago, but find baying at our heels.

8. The word translated *forgiving* (v. 32) does not simply mean to release from guilt, but to be gracious unto, be kind, be benevolent, pardon.

9. *Kind* — This word is usually used to describe God. It describes one who is virtuous, good, mild, pleasant.

10. The motive for Christian goodness is different from that of worldly righteousness. Out in the world people are good because "it pays." They get something in return. We are good and forgiving toward our fellow men because God has forgiven us. We realize how much we are indebted unto God. We therefore forgive the small offences our neighbors commit against us.

Fact Questions

250. Name the six things mentioned in 4:31 that we are to put away from us.

251. Quote Ephesians 4:32 from memory.

EPHESIANS FIVE

Duties of Church Members — Continued

EPHESIANS 5 – (Duties cont.)

**B. WALK AS BECOMETH SAINTS --
4:17-5:20**

1.

1. Practical Exhortations, 4:24-5:2

2. Walk As Children Of Light; 5:3-14

   a. Things children of light do not do; 5:3-8

   b. Things children of light do; 5:9-14

3. Walk As Wise Men; 5:15-20

**C. SUBJECT YOURSELVES ONE TO
ANOTHER — 5:21-6:9**

1. Husbands and Wives; 5:22-23

Text (5:1, 2)

Be ye therefore imitators of God, as beloved children; 2 and walk in love, even as Christ also loved you, and gave himself up for us, an offering and a sacrifice to God for an odor of a sweet smell.

Thought Questions (5:1-2)

269. What are we told about God's actions in 4:32 that we are here urged to imitate?
270. Which would God prefer, learning and greatness, or a child-like spirit? Can we have both?
271. What does it mean to *walk* in love?
272. Is there any difference between an *offering* and a sacrifice? Explain any difference.
273. What Bible incidents does the expression *an odor of a sweet smell* bring to your mind?

Paraphrase

1. Seeing that God in Christ has forgiven you, be ye therefore imitators of God's forgiving mercy as beloved children who imitate the actions of their parents.
2. And live your lives in a disposition of love, even as Christ loved you, and gave himself up for you when he died on the cross, and made himself an offering and a sacrifice for an odor (savor) of a sweet smell unto God.

Notes (5:1, 2)

1. Many types of offerings in the Old Testament are called "a sweet savor (odor) unto the Lord": the burnt offering (Leviticus 1:9, 13), the meal (meat) offering (Leviticus 2:3, 9), offering of first fruits (Leviticus 2:12, 16), peace offerings (Leviticus 3:5, 16), and sin offerings (Leviticus 4:21). The trespass offering is not so described.

   Noah offered up his offering unto the Lord after the flood, and the Lord "smelled the sweet savor" (Genesis 8:21). The critics have had much sport out of belittling such descriptions of God as if He were in human form (anthropomorphisms). But if the Scriptures say that God "smelled the sweet savor," we are not so wise that we can describe what God did any more accurately. The important thing is that the offering pleased the Lord and made the worshipper accepted. Like the people of ancient times, we sorely need

149

an offering that will be accepted of and well-pleasing to God. We are a people of unclean hands, minds and lips. We thank God that Christ is our sacrifice and odor of sweet smell, and that through His sacrifice we may be accepted by God.

2. The offering of Christ goes up to God for us in two respects:
   (1) A *sacrifice* for our transgressions. We deserve to die. Christ's death is a substitute for our death. He bore the punishment which we justly deserve to bear.
   (2) An *offering* to be presented when the transgression has been put out (or expiated), as an act of worship.

Fact Questions

252. Whom are we to imitate? In what way are we to imitate Him?
253. Christ gave Himself up for us as two things. Name them.

Previewing in Outline Form (5:3-20)

3. Walk as children of light. 5:3-14.
   a. Things the children of light do not do. 5:3-8a.
      (1) Do not even name vices as if they were becoming to saints. 5:3-6.
         (a) Those who partake in vices have no inheritance in the kingdom. 5:5.
         (b) The wrath of God comes upon those who disobey. 5:6.
      (2) Do not become partakers with the sons of disobedience. 5:7-8.
         (a) This they once did when they were darkness. 5:8.
         (b) They are now light in the Lord.
   b. Things the children of light do. 5:8b-14.
      (1) Walk as children of light, producing the fruit of the light. 5:8b-9.
      (2) Prove what is well-pleasing unto the Lord. 5:10.
      (3) Reprove the works of darkness. 5:11-14.
         (a) Have no fellowship with them. 5:11.
         (b) Their deeds are too shameful to speak of. 5:12.
         (c) Reproof makes manifest the works of darkness. 5:13.
         (d) A call to those in darkness. 5:14.
4. Walk as wise men. 5:15-20.
   a. Walk carefully. 5:15.

b. Buy up the time. 5:16.
c. Have the good sense to understand the Lord's will. 5:17.
d. Be not drunk with wine. 4:18a.
e. Be filled with the Spirit. 5:18b-20.
   (1) Speaking to one another in psalms, etc. 5:19a.
   (2) Singing and making melody. 5:19b.
   (3) Giving thanks always. 5:20.

Text (5:3, 4)

3 But fornication, and all uncleanness, or covetousness, let it not even be named among you, as becometh saints; 4 nor filthiness, nor foolish talking, or jesting, which are not befitting: but rather giving of thanks.

Thought Questions (5:3, 4)

274. If we are not to name fornication, uncleanness, etc., why does Paul name them?
275. Is covetousness as bad as fornication?
276. Why is jesting forbidden? Is all humor wrong? What do people often make jests about?
277. What does *befitting* mean?
278. What is one type of speech that is always befitting?

Paraphrase

3. Seeing that Christ loved us and gave himself up for us, flee fornication, lustful unclean living, greedy desires to have more, and such things. Do not even mention them. For it is becoming to saints not to speak of them. Mention them only to condemn.

4. Also shun base and lewd conduct, foolish talking, and jests with double meanings, for these things do not come up to the level of the Christian. But giving of thanks is always befitting.

Notes (5:3, 4)

1. *Jesting* refers to speech that is nimble-witted, or easily turned, especially toward a bad meaning. So often the jesting of the world is based on double meanings. Jokes are formed that can be taken with two meanings, one harmless, the other shady. Some comedians think that they are not funny unless they utter a few such jokes.

2. *Befit* means "to come up to, or to have arrived at, or to reach to." Many things are far below the Christian, and he must hold them in abhorrence. He avoids acting self-righteous, but he keeps himself from the evil one.

Fact Questions

254. Name the six things that are forbidden in 5:3-4.

Text (5:5-7)

5 For this ye know of a surety, that no fornicator, nor unclean person, nor covetous man, who is an idolater, hath any inheritance in the kingdom of Christ and God. 6 Let no man deceive you with empty words: for because of these things cometh the wrath of God upon the sons of disobedience. 7 Be ye not therefore partakers with them;

Thought Questions (5:5-7)

279. Do not many people consider sexual vice rather a casual thing, also a harmless diversion? Is it really an inconsequential thing?
280. Why is the covetous man called an *idolater?*
281. What is the kingdom of Christ and God? Can a man outwardly appear to belong to the kingdom, and yet have no inheritance in it?
282. What are *sons of disobedience?* (Compare 2:2.)
283. Why are words which attempt to excuse immorality and covetousness called *empty words?*
284. When does the wrath of God come upon those who disobey?

Paraphrase

5. You must obey the command to abstain from fornication, filthiness, covetousness, etc., for you know this with certainty by the light of the Gospel (v. 8) that no fornicator, nor unclean person, nor covetous man, who is really an idolater because he trusts in his riches, has any inheritance in the kingdom of Christ and God, which is the church.

6. Let no one deceive you with words that sound wise, but are empty of truth, saying that immorality and love of money are relatively harmless things. For on account of these sins the wrath of God has come and will come on those who practice them.

7. Wherefore, be not joint-partakers in their crimes, lest you share also in their punishments.

Notes (5:5-7)

1. You may be fellow-partakers with the saints (3:6), but you must not be fellow-partakers with those who are immoral and covetous. Evil companionships corrupt good morals (I Corinthians 15:33).

2. Note the reference to the *wrath of God* in verse six. Some people have said that the God of the New Testament is a God of love, in contrast to the God of the Old Testament who is a God of wrath. There is only one God, and He is the same in both the Old and New Testaments. The *wrath of God* is plainly taught in the New Testament, as it is in the Old. Those who desire to reject Christ should carefully consider the terrors of God's wrath. Let no clergyman, sociologist, professor, psychologist, or anyone else deceive you by saying that you can practice sin and not suffer God's wrath.

3. Justin Martyr (about A.D. 150) wrote: "We who were formerly the slaves of lust now only strive after purity; we who loved the path to riches above every other, now give what we have to the common use, and give to everyone that needs; we who hated and destroyed one another, now live together, and pray for our enemies, and endeavor to convince those who hate us without cause, so that they may order their lives according to Christ's glorious doctrine, and attain to the joyful hope of receiving like blessings with ourselves from God, the Lord of all."

Fact Questions

255. What do fornicators and covetous men absolutely not have?
256. What comes upon those who are sons of disobedience?
257. What is the covetous man called?

Text (5:8-10)

8 for ye were once darkness, but are now light in the Lord: walk as children of light 9 (for the fruit of the light is in all goodness and righteousness and truth), 10 proving what is well-pleasing unto the Lord;

Thought Questions (5:8-10)

285. What relationship are the children of light to have with the sons of disobedience? (Compare 5:7.)
286. Is there any difference between being darkness and being *in* darkness? Which did Paul say that we once were?

287. In Whom are we light? Does the world's wisdom add light to our nature?

288. How can light have children, so that we become *children of light?* (Compare I John 1:5.)

289. Is it possible to be light in the Lord, and not be good, righteous, and truthful? Why or why not? (See verse nine.)

290. What does *proving what is well-pleasing unto the Lord* mean? How can we do this?

Paraphrase

8. Be not fellow-partakers with those who are disobedient to God. For in the Lord Jesus you are now transformed to become light, instead of being part of the darkness of this world which once you were. Walk therefore as children of light.

9. To do this, you must walk in goodness, righteousness, and truth, for such as the fruits of the light.

10. As you walk as children of light, you shall be testing and proving the will of God, proving both to yourselves and to those who see you that that which is well-pleasing to the Lord is best for all mankind.

Notes (5:8-10)

1. The reading, *fruit of the light,* in 5:9 is preferable and more accurate than *fruit of the Spirit,* as given in the King James Version.

2. *Children of light* is practically the same expression as *children of God,* for God is light (I John 1:5).

3. Before our conversion we were actually darkness, not just *in* the dark. Now we are actually made to be light, and are not just *in* the light. As a magnet can rub off its magnetism onto another piece of iron and transform it into another magnet, so we become light as we are in contact with God and Christ. (See John 8:12.)

4. The world needs to see people believe in Christ and obey Him, for such people are testing and proving that that which is well-pleasing to God is best for all mankind. We are told several times in the Bible to prove (or test) that which is well-pleasing to the Lord (Romans 12:2; I Thessalonians 5:21; Malachi 3:10). God invites (and even dares) you to test Him, and see for yourself. No one who has ever given God an honest trial has said that God disappointed him.

Fact Questions

258. According to 5:8, what were we before conversion?
259. In what is the fruit of the light?
260. What will the children of light prove?

Text (5:11, 12)

11 and have no fellowship with the unfruitful works of darkness, but rather even reprove them; 12 for the things which are done by them in secret it is a shame even to speak of.

Thought Questions (5:11, 12)

291. How far can we go in avoiding wicked people, in order that we may have no fellowship with the works of darkness (I Corinthians 5:9-10)?
292. Why are the works of darkness called *unfruitful?* Do they not bear bad fruit?
293. What does *reprove* mean? Is it enough just to ignore evil?
294. Why are the deeds of darkness done in secret?
295. How can we reprove deeds if they are too shameful even to speak of?

Paraphrase

11. As children of light, have no partnership with the works of darkness, such as the heathen ceremonies of Diana; for these works of darkness bear no desirable fruit, and bring eternal death to those who partake of them. Rather, expose, reprove, and convict them.

12. For the impure and wicked actions which are done by them in secret places and in darkness are so abominable that it is a shame even to speak of them, except to condemn.

Notes (5:11, 12)

1. The phrase *have fellowship with* was an expression used by the Greeks to denote participation in their religious rites and mysteries. Paul wanted the disciples to have nothing in common with these.

2. *Reprove* means to convince or convict. It is not enough to ignore evil. We must expose it in such a way that people will not be misled by it.

3. While Paul may have had primary reference to the heathen mysteries of his time as being the *works of darkness*, the workers of iniquity in the 20th century still work in darkness,

155

and the things they do in secret are still too shameful to speak of. (See John 3:19-21.)

Fact Questions

261. With what are we to have no fellowship?
262. What are we to do with the works of darkness (v. 11)?
263. Where do the workers of darkness do their deeds?
264. How shameful are many of the works of darkness?

Text (5:13)

13 But all things when they are reproved are made manifest by the light: for everything that is made manifest is light.

Thought Questions (5:13)

296. When does the light make evil things manifest?
297. Is everything that is exposed to the light made to *be* light? Are the wicked transformed into light just by being exposed to the light?

Paraphrase

13. Now all the works of darkness, when they are reproved, are made manifest by the light. For everything that makes manifest the wicked works of darkness is light. Therefore, when you reprove them, you show that you are light. (5:8)

Notes (5:13)

1. The King James translation of 5:13b reads: "Whatsoever doth make manifest is light." We much prefer this translation to that of the Revised Version given above. Our reason for preferring the King James translation here is that many wicked people that are exposed to the light merely run to their lair, and go "under cover," hiding, but not seeking to get right with God. Such people certainly do not become *light* just because the light has been turned upon them.

   However, anything that makes manifest the wicked works of darkness is light. The saints who reprove the works of darkness and make them manifest for everyone to see, are light (Ephesians 5:8).

2. The heathen called their mysteries *light,* and those who were initiated into the mysteries, *the enlightened ones.* But if these religious delusions had really been light, they would have revealed the ungodly deeds of their devotees.

156

We still use the phrase, "light on the subject," to describe information that makes things clear. But much that is called *light* is only darkness disguised as wisdom.

3. Paul had been sent to turn the Gentiles from darkness to light (Acts 26:18).

Fact Questions

265. What is the difference between the King James and the Revised Versions in this verse? Why is the King James Version preferable?

266. What is *everything* that makes manifest the works of darkness?

Text (5:14)

14 Wherefore *he* saith, Awake, thou that sleepest, and arise from the dead, and Christ shall shine upon thee.

Thought Questions (5:14)

298. Who says, "Awake"? Is this an Old Testament quotation?

299. How can we arise from the dead by our own choice? (See 2:1).

300. At what time in our life does Christ begin to shine upon us?

Paraphrase

14. Wherefore, because we are light and reprove the works of darkness, our work and call to the world is stated in the saying: "Awake, thou that sleepest (in the darkness of heathen ignorance), and arise from the dead (the state of death in which you lie in trespasses and sins), and Christ shall shine upon thee (with the light of truth)."

Notes (5:14)

1. This saying is not a quotation from the Old Testament. It recalls Isaiah 60:1, but is not a quotation of that verse. Perhaps it is a line from an old hymn, or some heretofore unrecorded saying of Christ or one of the apostles.

2. As the morning sun enlightens men aroused from sleep, so Christ enlightens those who rouse from the sleep of sin and turn unto God. When men are converted, they are enlightened (Hebrews 6:4).

3. Many will wake up from spiritual sleep only when they fall into the sleep of death. Like the rich man, they will be

157

aware for the first time of their actual condition (Luke 16:23-31; compare Psalm 73:17-30).

Fact Questions

267. What is the source of the quotation, "Awake, thou that sleepest"?
268. From what are the sleepers to arise?
269. When the sleepers awake, Who will shine upon them?

Text (5:15, 16)

15 Look therefore carefully how ye walk, not as unwise, but as wise; 16 redeeming the time, because the days are evil.

Thought Questions (5:15, 16)

301. Why does the fact that the days are evil make it necessary to be careful how we use our time?
302. What determines whether our walk is wise or unwise?
303. Is it really possible to redeem, or buy back, wasted hours and days in our past? If not, what does *redeeming the time* mean?
304. Has there ever been a time when the saints could truly say, "The days are good"?

Paraphrase

15. See then that you, upon whom Christ now shines, walk carefully, according to Christ's teachings, not as unwise men, but as wise,

16. making prudent use of every moment, so that by zeal and well-doing you shall purchase the time for the Lord's services. For the days are evil, and there are many temptations to use our time foolishly.

Notes (5:15, 16)

1. *Redeeming the time* does not carry the idea of living for Christ so energetically that we can buy back wasted hours and days of the past. That is impossible. Rather, it is the present moment that we are to redeem (or purchase). With zeal and well-doing as purchase money, we can buy up the moments so as to make them our own. Then on the day of judgment when we give account of the use of our time, it will be on the credit side of our account.

158

2. Beware of any inclination to call the days *good*. We still live in an *untoward generation* (Acts 2:40). The churches may have more members than ever before, but even with all these members the population has grown faster than the churches. Furthermore, much of our modern "churchianity" is only a form of godliness, and not the real thing. We shall never be able to make a paradise of this sin-cursed world until the Lord returns. Dark pictures are painted in the Scriptures of the condition of the world in the latter days (II Timothy 3:1-5; Matthew 24:37-39). There is no ground for confidence in any social gospel that thinks it can transform the whole world into a paradise. We have great confidence in the power of the gospel. But not all men living at any one time have ever accepted the gospel.

Fact Questions

270. How are we to walk, according to 5:15?
271. What is the mental condition of those who walk carefully?
272. What are we to be doing to the time? What does this mean?
273. What is the condition of the days (or times)?

Text (5:17)

17 Wherefore be ye not foolish, but understand what the will of the Lord is.

Thought Questions (5:17)

305. Is there any connection between the days being evil (5:16) and our being foolish?
306. How can we understand what the will of the Lord is?

Paraphrase

17. Because the old days are evil, and are filled with great temptations, we must constantly beware of foolish, ungodly, time-wasting conduct. Instead, let us keep before our minds at all times that which is the will of the Lord, namely to abstain from all the works of darkness.

Fact Questions

274. What are we not to be, according to 5:17?
275. What are we to understand?

Text (5:18-20)

18 And be not drunken with wine, wherein is riot, but be filled with the Spirit; 19 speaking one to another (or, to yourselves) in psalms, and hymns and spiritual songs, singing and making melody with your heart to the Lord; 20 giving thanks always for all things in the name of our Lord Jesus Christ to God, even the Father

Thought Questions (5:18-20)

307. Can you think of any similarities between the effects of wine and of the Spirit? What difference is there in their effects?

308. What is the *riot* which is connected with the use of wine?

309. What is the difference, if any, between a *psalm*, a *hymn*, and a *spiritual song?*

310. Does the command to use psalms suggest that we ought to make a greater use of the Old Testament Psalms than most of us do nowadays?

311. Is the act of "giving thanks" connected with the singing?

312. Why give thanks in the name of Jesus Christ? Are we so utterly unworthy that we cannot even offer thanks to God except through the name of Jesus?

Paraphrase

18. And be not drunken with wine, as the heathen do in their rituals and revelries, for in wine comes debauchery of manners (fornications, brawlings, riots); but rather be filled with the Holy Spirit.

19. Instead of singing lewd songs, be speaking to one another with psalms such as David wrote, and hymns, and spiritual songs, thus singing and making melody with your heart to the Lord;

20. giving thanks also at all times for all things that befall you, whether pleasant or hard, offering the thanks through the mediation of the Lord Jesus Christ to God, the Father.

Notes (5:18-20)

1. The *riot* that comes through wine drinking refers to the loose type of behavior brought on by wine. The word *riot* (in a

160

the prodigal son when he left his father's home (Luke 15:13; compare Luke 15:30).

slightly different form) is used to describe the activities of

2. There are some similarities between the effects of wine and the effects of being filled with the Spirit. The apostles were accused of being filled with wine; (cp. Acts 2:1-13). Similarities between the effects of wine and the Spirit:

(1) Both afford satisfaction from without.
  a. The satisfaction of wine proves to be a mockery. Though it promises escape from reality, it only pulls one down into greater misery (Proverbs 20:1).
  b. The satisfaction furnished by the Spirit never brings regrets.

(2) Both bring feelings of joy.
  a. Wine produces a temporary exhilaration (Esther 1:10).
  b. Joy is a fruit of the Spirit, but it is not just a temporary blessing (Galatians 5:22).

(3) Those who are filled with either the Spirit or with wine always attract attention. Those filled with the Spirit are usually noticed at once because of their good behavior, and what they talk about.

(4) Both wine and the Spirit bring out a person's true, but sometimes hidden, character.
  a. Wine brings out all the bad character, the hidden hoards of wickedness, removing the restraints of conscience, so that lust, pride, and meanness are brought out into the open.
  b. The Spirit brings out hidden treasures of goodness. We have seen many cases where the Holy Spirit brought out fine hidden talents that people hardly knew they had.

3. Some have suggested that the command to speak to one another may refer to singing alternately (or antiphonally), a custom which was early practiced in the church.

161

The Revised Version margin translates 5:19a, "speaking to yourselves" in psalms, etc. This reading would suggest that we are to have so much of the Spirit and the music of Zion in our souls that we will speak to ourselves with spiritual music. It is very fine for people to be humming, or whistling, or singing some spiritual song to themselves.

4. Thayer's Greek-English Lexicon tells us that *psalms* were songs which took their general character from the Old Testament psalms, though not limited to them. *Hymns* are praise to God. *Spiritual songs* refer to any type of song, whether of praise or on any other subject.

5. Besides singing, another action of those who are filled with the Spirit is giving thanks always for all things. We can thank God by singing, but thanksgiving is not limited to that which is sung. We can even thank God for our tribulations.

It is a humbling thought, but this verse suggests that we are so unworthy that we cannot approach God, *even to thank Him,* except in the name of Christ.

Fact Questions

276. Paul says, "Be not drunken with wine, wherein is................."
277. With what are we to be filled, rather than being filled with wine?
278. With what three types of music are we to speak one to another?
279. What are *psalms?*
280. With what are we to sing and make melody?
281. Through Whom are we to give thanks?

Previewing in Outline Form (5:21-33)

C. Subject yourselves one to another. 5:21-6:9.
1. The command. 5:21.
2. Wives and husbands. 5:22-33.
    a. Wives to be subject unto husbands. 5:22-24, 33b.
        (1) As unto the Lord. 5:22.
        (2) The husband is head of the wife. 5:23.
        (3) The wife is to be subject to the husband as the church is to Christ. 5:24.
        (4) The wife is to fear her husband. 5:33b.
    b. Husbands to love their wives. 5:25-33a.
        (1) As Christ loved the church. 5:25-27.
            (a) He gave himself up for it. 5:25-27.
                ((1)) That He might sanctify it.
                ((2)) That He might present the church to Himself.
            (b) He nourishes and cherishes it. 5:29b-30.
            (c) The first marriage contained a mystery regarding Christ and the church. 5:31-32.
        (2) As their own bodies. 5:28-29a, 33a.
            (a) He that loves his wife loves himself. 5:28b.
            (b) No man ever hated his own flesh. 5:29a.
            (c) Each to love his own wife as himself. 5:33a.

Text (5:21)

21 subjecting yourselves one to another in the fear of Christ.

Thought Questions (5:21)

313. What is the virtue of being subject one to another?
314. If everyone is subject to everyone else, who will have authority?
315. What does the fear of Christ have to do with our being subject to one another?

Paraphrase

21. With respect to your duties one to another, you must be subjecting yourselves to one another, according to the various relationships in which you stand to one another. And this you must do because you fear the authority of Christ who has appointed these relationships.

Notes (5:21)

1. This verse begins a new section in the outline entitled, "Subject yourselves one to another." The general principle is laid down in this verse that we must be subject to one another; then in the development that follows it becomes obvious that what is meant is that we are to be subject according to the various positions we occupy in life. Specifically, the wife is to be subject to the husband, the child to the parent, and the slave to the master.

2. The duty to be *subjecting yourselves one to another* might appear to be parallel to *giving thanks* in 5:20. However, the matter of subjecting ourselves occupies such a long section in the text (it goes to 6:9), that we list it as a separate duty.

3. We do have ranks and positions of required subjection in this world. A Communist state where everyone is supposed to be perfectly equal is a slave state. Unless we are willing to be subject where subjection is proper, chaos will result.

4. Many of the Christians in the first century had unbelieving husbands, parents, or masters. The Christians were not to get unwarranted ideas of freedom and independence, and begin to disregard legitimate authority over them.

Fact Questions

282. What is the heading of section 5:21-6:9 in the outline?

Text (5:22-24)

22 Wives, *be in subjection* unto your own husbands, as unto the Lord. 23 For the husband is the head of the wife, as Christ also is the head of the church, *being* himself the saviour of the body. 24 But as the church is subject to Christ, so *let* the wives also *be* to their husbands in everything.

Thought Questions (5:22-24)

316. Do women have to be subject to men generally, or just to their own husbands?

317. Does the husband have authority to lord it over his wife, and force her to be in subjection?

318. Has the emancipation of women gone so far that they are no longer in subjection as the Scriptures' command? Should we have scrapped the phrase "love, honor, and obey," from the marriage vows?

319. What lesson should husbands learn from the fact that Christ's headship over the church is accompanied by His being Saviour of the body?

320. Is the husband to be regarded as omniscient (all-wise) as the Lord? How can the wife be a helper, and yet be in subjection?

321. Is there any limitation upon the authority of the husband over the wife? How far does "Be subject in everything" go?

Paraphrase

22. Considering the duties of mutual subjection in particular, wives, be subject to your own husbands in the same manner that you are subject to the Lord Jesus.

23. For the husband is the head of the wife and is entitled to direct her, even as Christ is the head of the church. However, Christ is a very kind head, being also the saviour of the body.

24. But as the church is subject to Christ in everything, let also the wives be subject to their own husbands in everything.

Notes (5:22-24)

1. Certainly no church member resents being in subjection to Christ. If husbands were what they should be, no wife should resent being in subjection to her husband. Remember that the man is not of the woman, but the woman of the man. The man was not created for the woman, but the woman for the man. (I Corinthians 11:8-9; Colossians 3:18; I Peter 3:1-6).

2. Nonetheless, when all reasonable causes for subjection (such as care, kindness, wisdom, etc.) are absent, the wife is still to be subject to the husband *as unto the Lord*. "Let her not leave her husband" (I Corinthians 7:13).

3. The wife's subjection does not mean that she has no moral or personal dignity. Her subjection is not servile. She is entitled to respect. She was created to be a helper, not a slave. Her service should not have to be done with fear and trembling. The husband has no authority to speak bitterly against her (Colossians 4:19). He has no authority to beat or abuse her.

166

Fact Questions

283. A woman's subjection to her husband is like her subjection to Whom?

284. What organic relationship does the husband bear to the wife that Christ also bears to the church (5:23)?

285. Christ is indeed head of the church, but what other relation does He have to the body (5:23)?

286. In what things are the wives to be subject to their husbands (5:24)?

Text (5:25, 26)

25 Husbands, love your wives, even as Christ also loved the church, and gave himself up for it; 26 that he might sanctify it, having cleansed it by the washing of water with the word.

Thought Questions (5:25, 26)

322. Whose example is a husband to imitate in his love for his wife?

323. Is the husband expected to give himself up for his wife?

324. Christ desired to *sanctify* the church (5:26). Is this something that is done at one time, or something that requires a lifetime? When and how are we sanctified? (See I Corinthians 6:11.)

325. To what does the *washing of water* refer? What reasons or supporting Scriptures can you give for your answer?

326. How does the Word go along with the washing of water?

Paraphrase

25. Husbands, love your wives, just as Christ loved the church so much that he was willing to give himself up and die for her.

26. Christ gave himself for the church that he might sanctify (purify and consecrate) her through the washing of water in baptism, and this is done wherever the word is taught.

Notes (5:25, 26)

1. "Wouldst thou that thy wife should obey thee as the church obeys Christ? Do thou then care for her, as Christ for the church, even if thou must lay down thy life for her — shrink not, shouldst thou suffer even this. Thou hast not yet matched all that which Christ hath done. For thou doest this after thou hast already won her, but he sacrificed himself for her

167

that turned away from him and hated him; and when she was thus disposed, he brought her to his feet not by threats, or insults, or terror, or any such thing, but by this great solicitude. So do thou conduct thyself toward that wife of thine. - - - Her that is the partner of thy life, the mother of thy children, the spring of thy joy, thou must not bind by terror and threats, but by love and gentleness." (Chrysostom)

2. The love of husband for wife is not that of passion, but of soul-love.

3. The church is to be sanctified as a result of Christ's sufferings. Because He died, we may be made righteous in the sight of God. The bride-groom relationship with Christ is the strongest possible reason for godly life on the part of the church.

4. The *washing of water* has been interpreted as referring to baptism by most commentators, both ancient and modern. (Compare Hebrews 10:22, and Titus 3:5) There have been some advocates of salvation by faith only who have tried to prove that the water mentioned here does not refer to baptism, and that Christian baptism has nothing to do with salvation or sanctification. Such interpretations are obviously not an effort to present what the Scriptures say, but to prove by the Scriptures the doctrines that one already believes.

5. It is plainly inferred in verse 26 that the entire church has been baptized.

6. *With the word* is literally translated *in word*. Wherever the Word of God has been taught, there Christ has cleansed the church by the washing of water. This plainly indicates that hearing and believing the Word must precede baptism.

     This interpretation of *with the word* is in accord with Mark 16:15-16, which describes the process of salvation as being (1) preaching the gospel (or the Word), (2) faith, (3) baptism, (4) salvation.

7. The tense (aorist) of *having cleansed* indicates that the cleansing is one specific action, rather than a progressive cleansing. This cleansing, or sanctification, takes place when we are baptized.

Fact Questions

287. What is the essential duty of husbands to wives?
288. How much did Christ love the church?
289. By what is the church sanctified?

290. How is the phrase *with the word* literally translated? What part does the Word have in our being cleansed?

Text (5:27)

27 that he might present the church to himself a glorious church, not having spot or wrinkle or any such thing, but that it should be holy and without blemish.

Thought Questions (5:27)

327. What did Christ do that He might present the church to Himself? (See 5:25-26.)

328. When will the church be presented to Christ?

329. What distinction would you make between a *spot* and a *wrinkle*? Applying these terms to the church, what might be called a *spot,* and what might be called a *wrinkle?*

330. Is the church to put on her own wedding garments, or is she to be adorned by the Lord (Revelation 19:7-8)?

331. When, if ever, will the church be without spot or wrinkle?

Paraphrase

27. Christ cleanses the church by the washing of water with the word for this purpose: that he may at his second coming present the church to himself, glorious, not in material garments, but in the beauty of righteousness, a church not having spot from external defilement, nor wrinkle from lack of care of her garments, but that it should be holy and without any blemish.

Notes (5:27)

1. The church shall be presented to Christ at His second coming (I Thessalonians 4:16-17).

2. The church in this world will never become faultless. But since salvation is a gift of grace, and not a matter of merit and moral perfection, the church will be caught up to her Bridegroom without spot or wrinkle, washed white in the blood of the Lamb.

   Without spot or wrinkle may refer to the perfection of the bodies of the saints, as well as to their spirits. Our present mortal bodies cannot inherit the kingdom of God. But when we are caught up with the Lord we shall have been transformed in body (I Corinthians 15:51-52).

3. It is pure delight to be joined to Christ as a bride to a husband. The joy of being married to Christ is rapturously pictured in the Song of Solomon and in Isaiah 62:4-5. We can call ourselves *Beulah,* which means *Married.*

Fact Questions

288. What kind of a church does Christ desire to present to Himself?
289. What defects is the church not to have when she is presented to Christ?

Text (5:28-30)

28 Even so ought husbands to love their own wives as their own bodies. He that loveth his own wife loveth himself: 29 for no man ever hated his own flesh; but nourisheth and cherisheth it, even as Christ also the church; 30 because we are members of his body.

Thought Questions (5:28-30)

332. Is the husband to love his wife in the same degree as he loves his own body? Or is he to love her as being a part of his body? What is the difference between the two ideas?
333. How can it be that he that loves his wife loves himself?
334. How does Christ *nourish* the church?
335. Is the church married to Christ, or just engaged to Him?

Paraphrase

28. Seeing that Christ loved the church so much that he gave himself up for it, men ought also to love their own wives as their own bodies. Indeed, the one who loves his wife loves himself, for she is as much a part of him as his own flesh.
29. And no one ever hated his own flesh, as a man would be doing if he did not love his wife. Rather, a man feeds his flesh to maturity and keeps it warm, just as Christ also nourishes and cherishes the church.
30. For we, the members of the church, are members of Christ's body, even as a husband and wife are one body.

Notes (5:28-30)

1. Husbands are not to love their wives in the same degree that they love their own bodies, but they are to love their wives as being one body with themselves. The wife is part of the

170

husband. The two are one flesh. The idea that the two are one makes love a compelling necessity, and not just a matter of condescension.

2. *Nourish* means to feed, feed to maturity, support, etc. Cherish means to warm, keep warm, to cherish with tender love.

3. It is a priceless thought to consider that Christ nourishes the church and cherishes her with the same warmth that a husband loves his wife. But indeed He does this, because we are members of His body, even as a husband and wife are one body. Christ nourishes the church with daily bread and food for the soul.

4. The phrase in the King James Version, *of his flesh and of his bones* is not found in the best and oldest manuscripts of the Bible. Therefore it is not included in the text of the Revised Version.

5. We may be members of the *body of Christ.* But the body (the church) does not exercise the authority of Christ. The head is the seat of all the authority. The body is subject in all things to the head. The church is not an authoritarian institution. (See notes on 1:20-23.)

6. The church is technically only engaged to Christ. The marriage supper of the Lamb is yet to come (II Corinthians 11:2; Revelation 19:7), but in Bible times the engagement was practically as binding as the marriage.

Fact Questions

290. Husbands are to love their wives as their own.............................
291. He that loveth his wife loveth ....
292. What two things does a man do for his own flesh that he should do for his wife?
293. Christ nourishes and cherishes the church because we are what (5:30)?

Text (5:31-32)

31 For this cause shall a man leave his father and mother, and shall cleave to his wife; and the two shall become one flesh. 32 This mystery is great: but I speak in regard of Christ and of the church.

Thought Questions (5:31-32)

336. What was the background of the original decree commanding that a man should leave his father and mother (Genesis 2:21-24)?

337. What was the original cause for which a man was commanded to leave his father and mother and cleave to his wife (Matthew 19:4-5)?

338. How could the original command to Adam have had reference to Christ and the church when the church was not in existence at that time?

339. What does the expression, *the two shall become one flesh* mean (Compare I Corinthians 6:16.)

340. Why is the relationship between Christ and the church called a *mystery?* Would you have ever imagined that Adam and Eve's marriage was designed to represent the relation between Christ and the church?

341. Can Christ be said to have left His Father for His wife?

Paraphrase

31. Now because God created mankind male and female, they were enjoined that the man should leave his father and mother and be inseparably united to his wife, being joined in fleshly union and in spiritual union.

32. This relationship between Adam and Eve contained a great mystery, a hidden meaning not originally made known, namely that their marriage relationship was not spoken only of them, but had reference to the relationship between Christ and the church.

Notes (5:31-32)

1. It is almost staggering to find that the original marriage of Adam and Eve was designed to represent the relationship between Christ and the church. But there are many points of resemblance:

    a. Eve was taken from the side of Adam. The church in like manner came from the side of Christ, for the church was purchased with His blood, which came from His side.

    b. Man was told to forsake parents for his bride. Christ forsook heaven to come to earth to win His bride.

    c. Adam loved Eve. Christ loves the church.

    d. There was only one wife for Adam (Malachi 2:15-16), only one bride, one church, for Christ (Ephesians 4:4).

172

e. The marriage of Adam and Eve was permanent for their lifetime. The marriage of Christ and the church will be permanent for their lifetime, eternity.

2. When we stop to think about it, it is hard to conceive of any reason why Eve should have been made from the rib of Adam unless God intended to illustrate the relation between Christ and the church. Eve could have been made from the dust as Adam was (and presumably the animals also). However, the appropriateness of the manner in which she was made becomes evident when we realize that it pictures the manner in which Christ produced the church.

3. The union between the Lord and His people was first conceived, then marriage was devised and employed as an illustration of the relationship. Marriage was not created first, and then later used as an illustration of the union of Christ and the church.

4. *Cleave to* means to "glue upon, glue to, join one's self closely to." When two pieces of wood are well glued together, the wood will break before the glue-joint does. Likewise in the marriage bond, the husband or wife should die before the marriage bond breaks.

5. The Vulgate (Latin Bible) says in 5:32 *sacramentum hoc magnum est,* which means, "This is a great sacrament." Upon this erroneous translation of "This mystery is great," the Roman church has proclaimed that marriage is one of the sacraments of the church. By controlling the marriages of its people, the Roman church holds an almost unbreakable grip upon the lives of its members.

Fact Questions

294. To whom, and when, was the statement first made, "For this cause shall a man leave his father and mother"?

295. What is the significance of the verb, *cleave?*

296. The application of Genesis 2:24 to Christ and the church is called a great ....

Text (5:33)

33 Nevertheless do ye also severally love each one his own wife even as himself; and *let* the wife *see* that she fear her husband.

Thought Questions (5:33)

342. Does the fact that Genesis 2:24 has reference to Christ and the church exclude its application to husbands and wives?

343. What degree of fear is a wife to have toward her husband?

Paraphrase

33. Notwithstanding the fact that the original marriage decree was intended to show the relation of Christ and his church, its application to human marriage remains unaffected, and thus each must love his own wife as being part of himself, and likewise let the wife take care to reverence and obey her husband.

Notes (5:33)

1. Marriage is regulated by divine commandments. The husband MUST love his wife. The wife MUST be in subjection to her husband. They MUST cleave together as long as they both shall live. To do otherwise is sin.

2. The fact that Genesis 2:24 had reference to Christ and the church certainly does NOT exclude its application to husbands and wives.

3. See the notes on 5:28 concerning the identity of the wife with her husband, and the consequent necessity of the husband loving his wife as himself.

4. *Fear* — The wife is not expected to fear her husband as a slave fears a tyrannical master, but rather as the church fears Christ. This is a blend of respect, love, gratitude and subjection.

Fact Questions

297. Accordng to 5:33, the wife is to .... her husband.

EPHESIANS SIX
The Whole Armor of God

A ROMAN CENTURION

The staff (**vitis**) in his right hand was an emblem of office and was used to enforce discipline.

Previewing in Outline Form (6:1-9)

C. Subject yourselves one to another. 5:21-6:9

   3. Children and fathers. 5:1-4.

     a. Children to obey. 6:1-3.

       (1) This is right. 6:1.

       (2) This is commanded by the Law. 6:2a.

       (3) This commandment is accompanied with promises. 6:2b-3.

         (a) That it may be well with thee.

         (b) That thou mayest live long in the earth.

     b. Fathers. 6:4.

       (1) Provoke not your children to wrath.

       (2) Nurture them in chastening and admonition.

   4. Slaves and masters. 6:5-9.

     a. Slaves to be obedient. 6:5-8.

       (1) With fear and trembling. 6:5.

       (2) In singleness of heart.

       (3) As unto Christ.

       (4) Not in the way of eyeservice. 5:6.

       (5) As servants of Christ. 5:6.

       (6) Doing service with good will 5:7.

       (7) Knowing that we shall receive from the Lord that which we do. 5:8.

     b. Masters. 6:9.

       (1) Treat slaves as they are to treat you.

       (2) Forbear threatening.

         (a) Christ the Master of everyone is in heaven.

         (b) Christ will have no respect of persons.

D. Put on the whole armor of God. 6:10-20 conclusion; 6:21-24.

EPHESIANS

CHAPTER
SIX

C. SUBJECT YOURSELVES ONE TO ANOTHER

1. Wives — husbands 5:22-33
2. Children — Fathers 6:1-4
3. Slaves — Masters 6:5-9

D. PUT ON THE WHOLE ARMOR OF GOD 6:10-20

Conclusion 6:21-24

Text (6:1-4)

Children, obey your parents in the Lord: for this is right. 2 Honor thy father and mother (which is the first commandment with promise), 3 that it may be well with thee, and thou mayest live long on the earth. 4 And, ye fathers, provoke not your children to wrath: but nurture them in the chastening and admonition of the Lord.

Thought Questions (6:1-4)

344. What does *obey — in the Lord* mean? Does that mean that children are to obey only when the parents command that which is in harmony with the Lord's will? Are children capable of judging what is in harmony with the will of the Lord? Or does it mean that they are to obey because they are *in the* Lord, that is, Christians?

345. Would you think that the parents referred to in 6:1 were Christians? Are the children to obey whether or not the parents are Christians?

346. Often child "experts" refuse to admit the existence of unchangeable standards of right and wrong. Paul says that obedience to parents is right. What determines whether a thing is right or wrong?

347. What is the twofold promise attached to honoring father and mother? Is the honor due to parents limited to childhood obedience? Should it include care in old age (I Timothy 5:4)?

348. What was the original significance of the promise, *that thou mayest live long in the earth* (or land) (Deuteronomy 5:33; 6:2; 11:8-9)? Does the promise still have an application to us? How could a father provoke his child to wrath? What results can follow such provocation? (Compare Colossians 3:21.)

349. What is *chastening* and what is *admonition?* Is it possible to give chastening and admonition that is not *of the Lord?*

Paraphrase

1. Children, obey even your unbelieving parents, seeing that you are obligated to do this because you are in the Lord. For this is just.

2. The law commanded you, children, to honor father and mother with obedience, respect, and care. This is the first

commandment of the ten commandments with a specific promise.

3. These are the promises that were attached to the commandment: (1) that it may be well with you; and (2) that you may live long in the land of Canaan.

4. And you, fathers, do not provoke your children to boiling wrath by unreasonable demands, cruel treatment, and constant irritation. Rather, nourish them up to maturity with the instruction, chastisement, and affectionate persuasion which the Lord directs us to employ.

Notes (6:1-4)

1. Some children have been cruelly repressed by their parents, but far more have never been made to obey and respect their parents. The child that is not taught to obey parents has a head start on the road to delinquency, crime, and hell. "A Chicago judge made a study of 1000 cases of juvenile delinquency. In 97% of the cases the mother exercises no discipline; the father exercises none in 98% of the cases." (Gerstner).

2. Children are to obey *in the Lord*. It is most unlikely that Paul meant that children were to judge whether or not the things their parents commanded were in harmony with the Lord's will. Most children would not be capable of deciding such things. The duty of the child is to obey. Naturally, the Christian child or youth would refuse to sacrifice to an idol, or drink liquor, or do such things, even if told to do them by a parent. However, commands that could be disobeyed because they were obviously sinful would be very rare. *In the Lord* simply means *because you are in the Lord, or because you are Christians.* It has always been the duty of children who served the Lord to obey their parents.

3. Considering all that a parent does and sacrifices for a child, it is infinitely just (right) that the child should obey.

4. The second of the ten commandments has a rather general promise to those who obey it. But the fifth commandment, *Honor thy father and thy mother,* is the first and only one of the ten commandments with a specific promise. This promise was twofold:

(1) *That it may be well with thee.* Any child that obeys his parents will be spared many troubles and mistakes, and he will also be spared much chastisement: The Law per-

mitted the stoning of a rebellious child (Deuteronomy 21:18-21). This should impress us with the fact that God considers filial disobedience a terrible thing.

(2) *That thy days may be long in the land which the Lord thy God giveth thee.* This originally referred to the privilege of dwelling in the land of Canaan. God warned Israel that if they were disobedient they would be driven out of the land (Deuteronomy 28:36).

This promise also has a fulfillment in the present times. The child who obeys will probably have better health, safer habits, wiser ways, and certainly the blessing of God to lengthen and enrich his life.

5. Parents who are unreasonably strict with children often drive them from home into young, unwise marriages, or into juvenile gangs. No parents should tease or repress children until they are in a rage. Foolishness is indeed bound up in the heart of a child (Proverbs 22:15). The rod of correction is needed, and a child will not long resent just punishment. But unjust continuous abuse (corporeal or verbal) leads to exasperation and discouragement.

6. *Chastening* refers to training, education, chastisement. Parents are under divine responsibility to educate their children. Children are not ours just to enjoy and caress, but to train for this life and the life to come. Children grow up and thank their parents for their educational opportunities. Will they grow up and thank their parents for spiritual instruction? Or will they grow up thirsting for the Word of the Lord which their parents did not give to them (Amos 8:11-12)?

7. *Admonition* refers to exhortation, urging, warning. We not only need to teach children the truth, but to urge them to live by it. We notice the attitude of entreaty and exhortation in Proverbs 5:1; 6:1.

Fact Questions

298. What is the duty of children to their parents?
299. Children are to obey parents, for this is................
300. Which is the first of the ten commandments with promise?
301. What is the twofold promise to those who obey parents?
302. What are fathers not to do?
303. In what two matters are parents to nurture their children?

Text (6:5-7)

5 Servants, be obedient unto them that according to the flesh are your masters, with fear and trembling, in singleness of your heart, as unto Christ; not in the way of eyeservice, as menpleasers; but as servants of Christ, doing the will of God from the heart; 7 with good will doing service as unto the Lord, and not unto men:

Thought Questions (6:5-7)

350. Does the Bible condone slavery? Does it abolish slavery by executive order?

351. The servant is to render service unto the master as unto Whom?

352. Does the authority of the master extend over the slave's flesh, or soul, or both?

353. Is the slave to fear and tremble because of his master's authority, or the Lord's authority, or the authority of both?

354. What is *singleness of heart?*

355. What is *eyeservice?*

356. Whom do we serve when we serve our masters faithfully?

357. Is most slave-service rendered with good will?

Paraphrase

5. Bond-servants (slaves), obey those who are the masters over your bodies and flesh, with fear and trembling, lest you be justly punished for slothfulness and unfaithfulness, both by the master and the Lord. Serve the master with but a single purpose in your heart, that of pleasing him, just as you desire to please Christ.

6. Render service not just when the master is looking, as one who is concerned only about pleasing men, but, as slaves of Christ who do the will of God from a heart wholly dedicated to Him, render service faithfully.

7. Thus, unlike most slaves, you will serve your masters with good will, and will cheerfully do the service that they require as if you were doing service unto the Lord, and not unto men only.

Notes (6:5-7)

1. The *servants* referred to in these verses were bond-servants or slaves. (Compare Colossians 3:22-25.)

181

2. The gospel of Christ does not automatically cancel slavery, but it does completely change the estimation of the slave in the master's eyes. To the Romans, slaves were generally looked upon only as *things*. To Christian masters, they became *people*, and even *brothers* in the Lord, if the slaves were Christians. Naturally, the Christian masters treated their slaves differently than did the heathen masters. It is unthinkable that anyone would enslave or mistreat a brother.

Then also, Christianity changed the slave's estimation of his master. The service his master required became an opportunity to serve Christ, and to demonstrate the power of Jesus in his soul. He served with the usual fear and trembling lest he displease his master, but even more earnestly lest he displease the Lord who was expecting him to be a good slave.

No doubt, when a slave became a Christian, and began to serve the master more faithfully, more cheerfully, more dependably, and more graciously, the master would wonder why. What an opportunity this would be for the slave to testify to the master concerning what Christ had done for him.

3. *Eyeservice* is either (1) service that is done only when the master has his eye on the slave, or (2) service done in such a poor way that it will only bear looking at, but not testing.

Fact Questions

304. What are the *servants* that are referred to in 6:5?

305. The masters of Christian slaves were masters over what part of them?

306. Whom was the slave serving when he served his master well?

Text (6:8)

8 knowing that whatsoever good thing each one doeth, the same shall he receive again from the Lord, whether *he be* bond or free.

Thought Questions (6:8)

358. If we have done some good thing, when shall we receive that same good thing again from the Lord?

359. Give some example, if you can, of how the Lord may give unto us the same good thing we have done for someone else.

360. How does the fact that we shall receive from the Lord the good things we have done have a beneficial effect both on the slave and his master?

Paraphrase

8. Knowing this, ye slaves, that whatsoever good work each man does, though he receives no reward from any masters on earth, he shall receive a reward from Christ on the day of judgment for this good work, and the reward will be in the same degree and kind as the good thing that he has done. This recompense shall be made to every saved man, whether he be presently slave or freeman.

Fact Questions

307. If we do not receive a reward for good works on earth, when and where will we receive our reward?
308. How will our rewards from the Lord be apportioned?
309. What difference will it make when the rewards are given whether we are free or bond?

Text (6:9)

9 And, ye masters, do the same things unto them, and forbear threatening; knowing that he who is both their Master and yours is in heaven, and there is no respect of persons with him.

Thought Questions (6:9)

361. What are the *same things* that the master must do toward the slave, as the slave toward the master? (Compare 6:5-8.)
362. Why should masters forbear threatening? Is it true that words cannot hurt anyone?
363. Who, and where, is the One who is Master of both the slave and his master?
364. Why would the warning that there is no respect of persons with Christ be especially needed by the slave master?

Paraphrase

9. And, you masters, exercise the same benevolent, conscientious acts toward your slaves that Christ requires of them to do toward you, not adding to their miseries by the terror of punishment, but leaving off threatenings, knowing that the Lord of both slave and master is in heaven on His

throne, and that in the judgment which Christ shall conduct upon His servants, He will respect no man's earthly rank or dignity, but will reward or punish everyone according to his deeds.

Notes (6:9)

1. The phrase, *forbear threatening,* carries the idea of moderating threats, or relaxing threats, or omitting threats. Threats often produce more terror, and hurt more deeply than stripes and lashings.

Fact Questions

310. What are the masters to do toward the slaves?
311. What are the masters to forbear?
312. Where is the one who is Master of both slave and master?
313. What attitude does the Master in heaven not have?

Previewing in Outline Form (6:10-20)

D. Put on the whole armor of God. 6:10-20.
  1. Exhortation to be strengthened. 6:10-13.
    a. Strengthened in the Lord. 6:10.
    b. Strengthened by putting on the armor. 6:11, 13.
    c. Strengthening necessary because our enemies are spiritual. 6:12.
  2. The armor described. 6:14-17.
    a. Girdle of truth. 6:14a.
    b. Breastplate of righteousness. 6:14b.
    c. Feet shod with preparation. 6:15.
    d. Shield of faith. 6:16.
    e. Helmet of salvaton. 6:17a.
    f. Sword of the Spirit. 6:17b.
  3. Exhortation to prayer. 6:18-20.
    a. At all seasons for all saints. 6:18.
    b. For Paul. 6:19-20.
      (1) That he might speak the right words. 6:19a.
      (2) That he might speak with boldness. 6:19b-20.

Text (6:10)

10 Finally, be strong in the Lord, and in the strength of his might.

Thought Questions (6:10)

365. From what source does Paul say we must get our strength?
366. How can we obtain the help available to us through the strength of God's might?

Paraphrase

10. Henceforth, my brethren, be strengthened by the access you have to divine help in the Lord, and by the mighty strength which God has made available to help you.

Notes (6:10)

1. The expression "finally" carries the idea of "For the remainder", or "henceforth".
2. "Be strong" is better understood in a passive sense, "Be strengthened," or "Be made strong".
3. Spiritual strength does not exist in us by nature, and it does not automatically and permanently remain ours when we have once gained it. Redeemed people need to feel dependence at every step.
4. Paul could say "Be strong" knowing that he had set an example for the Ephesians and knew every struggle they would have to face.
5. *Strength of his might* is an expression describing the power by which God strengthens us. Similar descriptions of His power are in 1:19 and 3:16. We can avail ourselves of the strength of God's might by putting on the armor of God described in 6:14-17, and by prayer.

Fact Questions

314. In Whom are we to be strengthened?
315. How is the power which God gives to aid us described?

Text (6:11-13)

11 Put on the whole armor of God that ye may be able to stand against the wiles of the devil. 12 For our wrestling is not against flesh and blood, but against the principalities, against the powers against the world-rulers of this darkness, against the spiritual *hosts* of wickedness in the heavenly *places*. 13 Wherefore take up the whole armor of God, that ye may be able to withstand in the evil day, and, having done all, to stand.

Thought Questions (6:11-13)

367. What is the *armor of God?* Is this the armor that God wears, or is it the armor that He provides to us?
368. What are *wiles?* Why does the devil use wiles? Is human strength sufficient to stand against the devil's wiles?
369. What is *flesh and blood?* Don't we have to contend with flesh and blood? Doesn't the devil employ flesh and blood to do his work?
370. How can we be *wrestling* while wearing armor?
371. How can we be wrestling with spiritual forces when we cannot see them?
372. Why is this world called *darkness* (Romans 1:21; Ephesians 4:18)?
373. Where do the wicked spiritual hosts dwell? How can they harm us from there?
374. What is the difference between *withstand* and *stand?*
375. What is the *evil day* in which we must be able to withstand?
376. After being fully armed and enabled to stand, what are we to do? Upon whom does this place responsibility?

Paraphrase

11. Put on the complete armor provided by God for us, so that, being fully protected, you may be able to stand firm against the treacherous tricks of the devil, by which he aims to destroy your soul.

12. It is absolutely necessary to be thus fully armed. For our struggle is not against human beings, flesh and blood, but against the very highest orders of evil angels, those with great power, those that rule over the idolatrous and sinful men in this world of darkness, against wicked spiritual hosts who inhabit the heavenlies, that is, the regions of the air, from whence they conveniently assault us and seek to get us to commit sin.

13. For this reason, that you wrestle with spiritual enemies, take up the complete armor which God has provided, that you may be able to stand against the assaults of the devil in the day of temptation. Then, having completed all of this preparation, stand with determination and steadfastness.

Notes (6:11-13)

1. The expression, *whole armor,* is a translation of the word which we transliterate *panoply.*

186

2. A Christian's own understanding and gifts do not sufficiently arm him. The Christian warrior must fight with weapons divinely provided.

3. Take the armor of God. Don't attempt to make your own.

4. Satan is a real being, filled with power, great knowledge, and great hate. Only those who make themselves fools by professing great wisdom deny his existence. (See note 6 on 2:1-3.)

5. Our battle with Satan is raging within us, and yet we are scarcely aware of it. The silence of the conflict is one of the perils of it. We are contestants, not spectators who can slumber as they contemplate the struggle.

6. Wiles are tricks, devices, "pits dug in unsuspected places". The devil does not leave us at conversion, but troubles, seduces, and besets us. As we had to depend on Christ to save us at the beginning of our Christian life, so we must still depend on Christ to carry us through. Our strength is in the Lord. As much as man dislikes to admit it, man alone is unable to cope with evil.

7. Here are some of the wiles of the devil:

   (1) Sin is presented as a virtue, or even as a religious act.

   (2) The vileness of sin is disguised under excuses, such as youth, old age, strong temptation, necessity to keep one's job, or to provide for one's family.

   (3) The hypocrisy of church members is pleaded as an apology for sin.

   (4) God's mercy is stressed and His Holiness and judgment ignored.

   (5) The individual is caused to think that he is strong enough to stand against sin (I Corinthians 10:12).

   (6) Christ is presented as saving us from sin's consequences rather than from sin itself.

   (7) We are told that the majority must be right, and that the saints are few in number and misfits in society.

   (8) We are lulled by the idea that we shall be accepted because of good deeds and offerings, and not because of our relationship to Christ.

8. We must STAND against the wiles of the devil. In other passages we are told to flee sin (I Corinthians 6:18). We should flee from temptations to do wrong, but stand fast in doing what is right.

9. Although we are told to put on armor, as if to fight on a battlefield, we are told that our struggle is also a *wrestling*. No armor is worn by wrestlers. While there is a mixing of figures of speech here, both the idea of wrestling and the idea of armor are important for our understanding.

   We, like Jacob, have to wrestle alone with the enemies of our souls, and with ourselves (Genesis 32:24-31; Hosea 12:3-4). Our struggle is described as *wrestling*, because it is an individual struggle and does not have the outward clangor of the battlefield. But it is fully as deadly.

10. The armor of God does not just defend us, but strengthens us.

11. If we do not overcome Satan, he will overcome us. It is a with Satan. Satan is mightier than we are: He is invisible, he is near us, he has strong help within us. We lose everything forever if he defeats us now.

12. We do not fight against flesh and blood, other human beings. Our weapons are not of the flesh (II Corinthians 10:4). We turn the other cheek. We oppose those who do Satan's work, not because we are against them, but because we are against Satan who works through them.

13. Concerning the *wrestling against the principalities*, any adult person knows that nothing goes right in this old world unless God or some good person works to make it go right. We would never know the reason for all of this trouble if the Bible did not tell us that all about us are unseen forces of evil, the devil and his angels, all organized into an efficient army with ranks and authorities. (See notes on 3:10.) Satan's forces dwell in the heavenly places, which refers to the regions of the air (Ephesians 2:1, 2; I Peter 5:8; Job 1:7). Satan is the prince of the power of the air, (and where do we not contact the air?) We do not see these spiritual hosts, but that is only because we, like the servant of Elisha, do not have our eyes opened to behold spiritual creatures (II Kings 6:15-17).

14. *This darkness* refers to our present world, which is predominently occupied by those who are darkened in their understanding. (Compare Colossians 1:13; Acts 26:18.)

15. The capacity for producing evil within the spiritual hosts of wickedness is only exceeded by their appetite to do evil.

16. *Withstand* carries the idea of standing against. One can *stand* when he has no adversaries, but he should still be standing after *withstanding* the assault of the enemy.

17. We must take up the whole armor of God. If we put on only five out of six pieces, we shall be vulnerable with an "Achilles heel." The word *all* in the expression *having done all,* means *quite all, the whole.*

18. The *evil day* is the season of temptation. This is usually brief, lasting only a *day.* But it is the crucial time.

Fact Questions

316. What are we to put on?
317. Against what are we to be enabled to stand?
318. What are *wiles?*
319. What are the *principalities and powers?*
320. Where are the spiritual hosts of wickedness?

ARMOR

The Romans copied their armor from the Greeks, but changed it considerably during the centuries. The Greeks used bronze for their armor, but the Romans used more iron. The Greeks showed their artistic nature in the design of their armor; Roman armor was less beautiful, but more practical.

The historian Polybius (about 200 B.C.) wrote a description of Roman armor in his time. His description indicates that the Roman armor at that time was much more like the armor of the Greeks than that used near the time of the apostles.

Polybius said that the Roman panoply consisted, in the first place, of a shield *(thureos),* and that along with the shield was a sword *(machaira).* Then next came two javelins *(hussoi)* and a helmet *(perikephalaia)* and a greave *(knemis).* The majority, when they had further put on a bronze plate, measuring a span every way, which they wore on their breasts, and called a heart guard *(kardiophulax),* are completely armed. But those citizens who were assessed at more than 10,000 drachmae wore instead, together with the other arms, *curiasses* made of chain mail.

Let us consider what the pieces of armor which Paul mentioned in Ephesians were like:

I. THE BREASTPLATE (or *curiass)*

This was the principal piece of defensive armor. The Greeks wore a breastplate made of two curved pieces of

189

bronze. One section covered the front of the body, and another the back. These were bound together at each side of the body. A wide bronze band passed over each shoulder, and was coupled to the front and back sections of the breastplate. The Greeks hung wide leather strips from the lower edge of the breastplate to form a sort of skirt. The Greek soldier did not protect his abdomen and thighs because he wanted to keep his movements free.

The original design for the Roman legionary's hooped *curiass* was borrowed from the Greeks, but the Romans remodeled it to suit their own fancy. Instead of making the breastplate in two large sections, they made it in hoops, which were wrapped around the body like ribs. These were actually supported by the leather tunic to which they were sewn. The hoops were hinged at the back and clasped in front. The shoulder pieces were made in four strips, less cumbersome than the single plate of the Greeks. The leather tabs at the bottom of the *curiass* were retained by the Romans, and they added others over the upper arms.

II. GIRDLE

The Roman soldier wore a military belt (Greek, *zoster* or *zone;* Latin, *balteus*). This secured the body armor at the waist and sometimes served as a sword belt. More often the sword was supported by a *baldric* over the left shoulder.

III. FOOTGEAR

The Greeks wore sandals and custom-tailored bronze greaves, which covered their ankles, shins, and knees. These greaves were so carefully formed that they required no straps to hold them in place. Goliath wore greaves of brass (I Samuel 17:6). The Greek word, *knemis,* used by Paul actually means a greave.

However, the Roman soldiers of Paul's time apparently wore greaves only rarely. They usually wore high-topped sandals, which we might call "boot-sandals." It would be much easier to make a long forced march in such footgear than in the greaves of the Greeks.

IV. HELMET

Helmets were of many styles. Some Greek helmets even had metal coverings over the face, leaving only the eyes exposed. Greek helmets were sometimes adorned with elegant plumes of horsehair.

The Roman legionary's helmet had reinforcing bars crossing one another at the crown of the head. At the crossing of the bars there was a ring to support the crest. Most Roman helmets had hinged cheek guards. The helmets of officers had plumes of feathers or other materials.

V. SWORD

In its heyday the Roman sword was about twenty-two inches long, double-edged, and perfectly straight, the point at quite an obtuse angle. It was worn on the right side, usually hanging from a sword belt (or *baldric*). Roman swords were made in Spain.

(Paul naturally omits reference to the Roman soldier's chief offensive weapon, the *pilum,* an iron-headed, thick-handled spear.)

VI. SHIELD

The legionary's shield was large and oblong, approximately 2½ feet by 4 feet. The corners were sometimes cut out. It was curved to fit the body. On its face was the insignia and the number of the legion to which its owner belonged. The shields were sometimes made of metal, and sometimes of wood covered on the outside with thick leather, which not only deadened the shock of a missile, but protected the frame of the shield from fire-tipped darts.

These 'fiery-darts" (*falarica*) were headed with lead, in or about which some combustible substance was placed and set aflame to destroy enemy defences.

The Romans and Greeks also used small circular shields (Greek, *aspis;* Latin, *clipeus*). But the shield to which Paul refers was the large door-like shield. In fact, its Greek name *thureos* (from *thura)* means *door*. The shield of faith is not a small protection, but a large and adequate one.

The Greeks used the large shields to make a solid wall of defence before them. They stood side by side with their shields before them, overlapping the edges. Their long spears were thrust before them. Since the spears were sometimes as much as 21 feet long, and even those carried by the sixth rank projected out well ahead of the front line of shields, any enemy faced a very prickly obstacle. This well illustrates that when Christians stand together, they have greater strength than when they stand alone.

GREEK HOPLITE (foot soldier)

A ROMAN CENTURION'S
HELMET

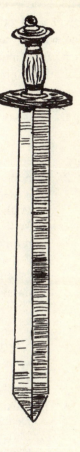

A ROMAN LEGIONARY'S
HELMET

A ROMAN
SWORD

THE WHOLE ARMOR OF GOD
(Ephesians 6:10-20)

This is a lesson which you can teach to children or adults. You will need other notes, illustrations, etc., but the following outline will be helpful. A useful visual aid is "The Christian Soldier" for flannelboard, by Helen Stephens Leonard, published by Christian Publications, Inc.

INTRODUCTION

1. Paul saw many Roman soldiers in his lifetime.
   a. A centurion escorted him to Rome (Acts 27:1).
   b. During his two years' imprisonment in Rome, he was chained to a soldier guard (Acts 28:16-20).
2. Paul observed the soldier's armor very carefully.
3. Paul thought about how essential a soldier's armor is.
   a. Without it he is only a civilian.
   b. With it he can defeat a dozen unarmed men.
4. Paul thought about how he was a soldier for Christ.
5. Paul thought about the terrible spiritual enemies of the Christian (6:11, 12).
6. Paul thought of the various means of protection that God has provided for the Christian. These he compares to the armor of a Roman soldier.

I. LOINS GIRDED WITH TRUTH

1. Describe how Roman armor protected the loins.
2. Football pants protect the loins of athletes.
3. Truth girds our loins.
4. The plain inference is that untruth is deadly.
   a. Denominational doctrines.
   b. Marrying out of the faith.
   c. Evolution, modernism.

II. BREASTPLATE OF RIGHTEOUSNESS

1. Describe the Roman breastplate.
2. The breastplate protects the heart. Bullet-proof vests are still used.
3. Righteousness and abstaining from vice (such as alcohol, tobacco, cursing, etc.) will protect your life from great harm.

III. FEET SHOD WITH THE PREPARATION OF THE GOSPEL

1. Describe Roman and Greek footgear.
2. George Washington's soldiers at Valley Forge had bleeding, shoeless feet. Such soldiers are nearly helpless. The church needs a bleeding heart for lost souls, but not bleeding, crippled feet.
3. Prepare yourself to march for Christ by memorizing Scriptures, collecting visual aids, reading good books.

IV. SHIELD OF FAITH

1. Describe the large door-like shields.
2. Describe the fiery darts.
3. Faith protects us from the fiery darts of doubt, despondency, discouragement, dread, disappointment, and death.

V. HELMET OF SALVATION

1. Describe Greek and Roman helmets.
2. Helmets are worn for protection and beauty, both in combat and on dress parade.
   a. Salvation protects (I Corinthians 10:13; I John 4:4).
   b. Salvation makes beautiful (Isaiah 61:3).

VI. SWORD OF THE SPIRIT (the Word of God)

1. Describe Roman swords.
2. Skill in handling the Word of God is powerful in both defense and offense.

VII. KEEP IN CONTACT WITH HEADQUARTERS BY PRAYER (6:18-20)

1. Walkie-talkies have helped in many battles.
2. Prayer keeps us in contact with heaven, and helps our fellow-warriors for Christ.

CONCLUSION

1. Too many churches are hospitals for wounded feelings, and not recruiting centers for soldiers of the cross.
2. Will you put on the gospel armor to battle for Christ?

Text (6:14-17)

14 Stand therefore, having girded your loins with truth, and having on the breastplate of righteousness, 15 and having shod your feet with the preparation of the gospel of peace; 16 withal taking up the shield of faith, wherewith ye shall be able to

quench all the fiery darts of the evil *one*. 17 And take the helmet of salvation, and the sword of the Spirit, which is the word of God.

(The article on Armor, page 256, and the lesson on page 262 will be helpful in considering this section.)

Thought Questions (6:14-17)

377. What similarities can you see between truth and a military girdle (or belt)?

378. Why is the breastplate a most important piece of armor? Why is righteousness like a breastplate?

379. In what ways is preparation like a soldier's footgear?

380. Why should we be in armor for conflict, if our gospel is a gospel of peace?

381. Name three things which you would consider as fiery darts of Satan.

382. What are the purposes of helmets? Why is salvation like a helmet?

383. Why is the Word of God called the *sword of the Spirit?* What part did the Holy Spirit have in the creation of this sword? its use? its effects?

Paraphrase

14. Stand therefore, having girded your loins about with the truth of the gospel, as soldiers are girded with the military belt; and having put on the breastplate of righteousness as a protection against the mortal injuries of sin.

15. And, like soldiers who prepare and protect their feet and legs with shoes and greaves, stand, having shod your feet with the preparation needed for preaching the gospel of peace.

16. In all your arming of yourself, take up the great shield of faith, the firm belief in the doctrines and promises of the gospel, with which you will be able to extinguish all the fiery darts of Satan, the evil one.

17. And take the helmet of salvation, as a protection and adornment to the soul; and take ye that sword of the Spirit, which is the word of God, that you may protect yourself and put your enemies to flight.

Notes (6:14-17)

1. Other passages referring to the gospel armor are I Thessalonians 5:8 and Romans 13:12.
2. *Girded with truth*: Too many people are girded with such "broadmindedness," that they are indifferent to the truth. Such lack of convictions is sickening to the Lord.
3. *Breastplate of righteousness*:
   "He is but naked though locked up in steel,
   Whose conscience with unrighteousness is corrupted."
4. *Gospel of peace*: We work for peace, even while fighting Satan. We maintain a peaceable spirit toward Satan's followers, while struggling against Satan within them. Peace is both a means and an objective in our warfare.
5. *Shield of faith*: To increase faith, it is necessary to study the Word of God diligently, since faith comes by hearing. Faith will stop and put out not some, but all of Satan's fiery darts.
6. Our *helmet of salvation* keeps us from the fatal effects of temptation, the fear of death, worldly terrors, envy of the rich, etc., so that such things will not pervert our imaginations.
7. The *sword of the Spirit,* the Word of God, sent Satan scurrying when Jesus used it in the wilderness, saying, "It is written" (Matthew 4:10-11).
   The sword of the Spirit must be wielded to do any good. It cuts deeply (Hebrews 4:12; Acts 7:54). It is both defensive and offensive. God's Spirit inspired the Word of God (II Peter 1:21). When the Word of God is preached, God's Spirit causes it to produce good fruit in the human soul. Sometimes the fruit is produced long after the Word is preached (Isaiah 55:10-11).
8. The *helmet,* pointing toward the skies, is a natural figure of the Christian hope and salvation directed toward a higher and better world.

Fact Questions

321. With what are our loins to be girded?
322. What is the Christian's breastplate?
323. With what is the Christian to be shod?
324. What is our shield?
325. From whom do fiery darts come at the Christian?
326. What is our helmet?

327. What is the sword of the Christian?
328. Quote Ephesians 6:10-17 from memory.

Text (6:18-20)

18 with all prayer and supplication praying at all seasons in the Spirit, and watching thereunto in all perseverance and supplication for all the saints, 19 and on my behalf, that utterance may be given unto me in opening my mouth, to make known with boldness the mystery of the gospel, 20 for which I am an ambassador in chains; that in it I may speak boldly, as I ought to speak.

Thought Questions (6:18-20)

384. Is armor enough to make a soldier? Why is there a necessity for prayer?
385. What is praying *in the Spirit?* (literally *in spirit*)
386. What is there about praying that requires *watching?*
387. For whom is prayer to be offered?
388. What was Paul's specific need in prayer?
389. Which was more important to Paul, his message or his personal welfare? How can you tell?
390. What is most unusual about an ambassador being in chains?

Paraphrase

18. Put on your armor with all prayers of devotion and request, praying thus at every season with earnestness of spirit, and not going to sleep, but watching and persevering in requests for all of the saints.
19. And especially do you watch in prayer in my behalf, that there may be given unto me the proper words when I open my mouth in defence before the judges, and in speaking to those who daily come to my house (Acts 28:30-31), that I may make known with boldness the mystery of the gospel (Ephesians 3:3).
20. In behalf of that gospel, I execute the office of an ambassador while bound by a chain. And I request your prayers that I may be made bold to speak the gospel as I ought to speak it.

Notes (6:18-20)

1. It is not armor and weapons alone that make a soldier. Without courage, a man in armor is no soldier. Therefore, prayer is needed.

2. *Prayer* is that which is addressed to God (emphasizing devotion), and *supplication* is seeking or asking (emphasizing need).

3. *Watching* means *not going to sleep*. We should be continuously alert to see needs that should be prayed about.

4. Praying *in spirit* probably means praying with earnestness and in a sincere way that will please the Spirit and be aided by the Spirit (Romans 8:26-27).

5. Prayer should be offered for all saints, and particularly for ministers and leaders. We must not become like Elijah who thought that he was the only one left in Israel that served the Lord (I Kings 19:10). The battle for the right is not the battle of one person alone. Therefore, we must pray for all the saints.

6. *Utterance* here refers to skill in speaking, the faculty of speech, saying the right words at the right time.

7. An ambassador from one sovereign government to the capital of another nation is a privileged inviolable man. It is unthinkable that an ambassador would be put in chains. Yet Paul thus stood, an ambassador from the kingdom of God, representing his sovereign in Caesar's court, bound with a chain. It is a strange and moving scene.

8. Concerning Paul's *chain*, Paul was tied to the soldier with a chain fixed on his right wrist, and fastened to the soldier's left arm. The chain was of such length that the two could walk together with ease, wherever the apostle's affairs called him. The soldiers who were thus chained to Paul no doubt received great benefit from the apostle's conversation and preaching, and some were doubtless won to Christ.

9. *Boldness* is the great need of ministers. Even Paul needed it. (Compare Acts 4:29.)

Fact Questions

329. What were the Ephesians to be doing while taking up the armor of God (6:18)?

330. In what were they to pray (6:18)?

331. When did Paul desire the Ephesians to pray (6:18)?

332. For whom were the prayers to be offered?

333. What did Paul wish the Ephesians to ask on his behalf?

334. What office did Paul fulfill in bonds?

Text (6:21, 22)

21 But that ye also may know my affairs, how I do, Tychicus, the beloved brother and faithful minister in the Lord, shall make known to you all things: 22 whom I have sent unto you for this very purpose, that ye may know our state, and that he may comfort your hearts.

Thought Questions (6:21, 22)

391. How do these verses explain the lack of personal references in Ephesians?
392. *THE INTERPRETER'S BIBLE* says that these verses were taken down almost word for word from Colossians 4:7-8, and were certainly set down with that passage before the writer's eyes. Do you agree? Why or why not?
393. Why might the Ephesians have been in need of some comforting concerning Paul's affairs?
394. Check your Bible cross-references, or your concordance, concerning Tychicus. What else do we know about him?

Paraphrase

21. Now that you Ephesians may also know what things have happened to me and what I am doing, I have sent Tychicus unto you, who is a brother greatly beloved for his many excellent qualities, and also is a faithful minister in the Lord, who will make known to you all things concerning me.
22. I am sending him for this specific purpose that you may know our affairs, and that he may comfort and exhort your hearts by the news of how God has used me even in my imprisonment.

Notes (6:21, 22)

1. See Introduction, Section VII, concerning why Paul sent Tychicus with the personal news, rather than including it in this letter, as he did in numerous other letters.
2. Tychicus is mentioned in Acts 20:4, Colossians 4:7, II Timothy 4:12, and Titus 3:12. Tychicus was from Asia (Ephesus). Paul calls him a beloved brother, faithful minister, fellow-servant. Paul sent him on several missions, and he did the work with earnestness and ability. He travelled with those who bore the offering for the poor of Judea. We wish we knew more about Tychicus. God has countless such fine workmen in His kingdom, about whom little is

known, but when God shall render unto them according to their works, then shall we know them better (and they shall know us better).

Fact Questions

335. Who was sent to inform the Ephesians of Paul's personal affairs?
336. How (two ways) does Paul describe Tychicus?
337. What purposes did Paul have in mind for the Ephesians in sending Tychicus (6:22)?

Text (6:23, 24)

23 Peace be to the brethren, and love with faith, from God the Father and the Lord Jesus Christ. 24 Grace be with all them that love our Lord Jesus Christ with *a love* incorruptible.

Thought Questions (6:23, 24)

395. What word in this benediction is found in the close of every one of Paul's epistles (Romans 16:20; I Corinthians 16:23; etc.)? What does this word mean? (See notes on 1:6.)
396. What would be the benefit of faith accompanying love?
397. What kind of love is *incorruptible* love? Do you have such love?

Paraphrase

23. To my brethren at Ephesus whom I have known, and to the faithful in Christ Jesus whose faces I have not seen, I pray that you may have peace, and mutual love with true faith that will preserve the love, from God the Father and the Lord Jesus Christ.
24. May the favor of God be with all them who love our Lord Jesus with incorruptible sincerity.

Fact Questions

338. What three things does Paul wish for the Ephesians in 6:23?
339. What did Paul wish for all those who love the Lord Jesus (6:24)?
340. What type of love did the Ephesians need to have?

SPECIAL STUDY: DID CHRIST GO TO HELL?

"Now that he ascended, what is it but that he also descended first into the lower parts of the earth?" Ephesians 4:9.

Some people have thought that during the time between Christ's death on the cross and His resurrection, He went down into hell (or Hades) to preach to the people there, and to bring out the saints of Old Testament times who could not previously be taken into God's presence because no atonement price had been paid for their sins.

THE INTERPRETER'S BIBLE says of Ephesians 4:9 that it is certainly a reference — the earliest in Christian literature — to the descent of Christ into Hades.

The Apostles' (?) Creed says, "He (Christ) descended into hell." This doctrine is elaborately set forth in the *Gospel of Nicodemus,* an apocryphal gospel, which, according to the general consensus of scholars, was composed in the fifth century.

Those who accept this doctrine maintain that such references as I Peter 3:19; 4:6, Ephesians 4:9; and Matthew 27:52-53 support it.

However, there is much disagreement as to WHAT Christ may have done in hell (or really, *Hades,* the unseen world of all the dead). According to the *Gospel of Nicodemus* (a highly imaginary legend), Christ, between the time He died and rose again, went down to Hades to rescue Adam, Noah, Moses, Isaiah, and all the other Old Testament saints. They were being kept away from God's presence until the time when Christ should die and make complete atonement for the sins of all mankind of all ages.

Such teaching as this contradicts Romans 3:25, which says that God *passed over . . . the sins done aforetime* during the time of His forbearance. Apparently the Old Testament saints were ushered into heaven when they died, even as we are. Elijah was taken into heaven (II Kings 2:1, 11), and apparently Enoch was also (Hebrews 11:5). We read that Abraham was accounted righteous by faith (Romans 4:3). If God accounted him righteous, why should he have been shut off from God in a prison? It is true that full payment had not yet been made for the sins of these people until Christ died. But Christ is the *Lamb of God, slain from the foundation of the world* (Revelation 13:8; 5:6). Therefore, in anticipation of that sacrifice, God *passed over* the sins of the Old Testament saints.

I Peter 3:19 tells of Christ preaching to those who were in prison. Therefore, some have understood that Christ preached to the *sinners* in *Hades,* such as those who had been disobedient in the days of Noah.

There are many unanswerable questions and objections to the idea that Christ preached to the sinners in Hades.

(1) Why did He preach JUST to the sinners who were disobedient in the days of Noah, as the text indicates? Other ages had many disobedient, lost people who would have needed Christ.

(2) WHAT could Christ have preached to them? Between His death and resurrection, Christ could not have preached the gospel. For the gospel consists of His death, burial, *AND RESURRECTION* (I Corinthians 15:1-4). We know that Christ was *raised* for our justification (Romans 4:25). Therefore, during the period between His death and resurrection, Christ could not have offered them justification. Did He, then, go to hell to taunt those who were lost?

(3) WHAT PURPOSE would Christ have had for going to Hades? It is certain that the wicked were offered no second chance (II Peter 2:5, 9). And the righteous with their sins *passed over* did not need to be rescued.

(4) WHAT RESULTS could Christ have expected from such a preaching expedition? No one doubts that one could hold a *hot* revival meeting in hell! Note how concerned the rich man in Hades was about his soul and the souls of his brothers (Luke 16:24-28). But note also that Abraham said it was impossible for the rich man to change his state. Christ did not raise the wicked dead from the graves, and He could not have preached justification to them until He arose Himself.

To test any interpretation of a difficult Bible passage, such as I Peter 3:19, three questions may be asked:

(1) Exactly what does the text say? Are we reading ideas into it that are not actually stated in the text?

(2) Does the interpretation contradict other more plain passages of Scripture? Does it harmonize with other Scriptures?

(3) Does the interpretation fit into the context of the passage, so as to make one harmonious teaching with what goes before and what follows?

Let us consider the doctrine that Christ went to preach in hell in the light of the three questions given above:

(1) The text says that Christ was put to death in His flesh; but that He was *quickened,* or made alive, in (His) spirit. The word *spirit* should not be capitalized here, as it is in the King James Version. The Greek text simply says, *in spirit,* rather than *in THE (Holy) Spirit.* Now we know that Christ's spirit never actually died, but went into Paradise (Luke 23:46). The spirit of Christ was quickened in the sense that it received an increased vigor and power after His sufferings in the flesh. Read I Peter 3:22 to see how His spirit was *quickened.*

In speaking of the spirit of Christ, which was *quickened,* Peter says that Christ also went in spirit and preached unto the spirits *in prison.* Just WHEN He preached is not clearly indicated here. From this verse alone one could not determine whether the spirits were in prison when Christ preached to them, or were in prison when Peter wrote this letter, which was many years later.

(2) The doctrine that Christ preached to sinners in Hades contradicts Peter's own writings. II Peter 2:4-5, 9: "For if God spared not the angels that sinned, but cast them down to Hell *(Tartarus),* and delivered them into chains of darkness, to be reserved *unto judgment,* and spared not the old world, but saved Noah the eighth person (with seven others) - - - the Lord knoweth how to deliver the godly out of temptations, and to *reserve the unjust unto the day of judgment* to be punished." These verses positively rule out the doctrine that Christ offered these sinners of ancient times a second chance (and we can conceive of no other reason why Christ should have preached to them).

Furthermore, the doctrine contradicts Christ's statement in Luke 23:43 that He would be in Paradise after His death. Certainly the sinners who had been disobedient in the days of Noah were not in Paradise where Christ went.

(3) The thought of the whole passage, I Peter 3:17-4:2, is that it is better to suffer, if need be, in well-doing than to compromise with evil. (Note especially 3:17 and 4:1.) To prove this point, the sufferings of Christ are set forth

204

as an illustration. (See 3:18.) The glory that came to
Him after His sufferings (see 3:22) shows us that we
will also do well to endure sufferings patiently.

Question — Does the supposed preaching expedition
into Hades show that Christ's sufferings were rewarded?
And does it thus set forth His sufferings as an encouragement to us in suffering? The answer is *no* to both of
these questions. Since we know nothing whatever about
what this supposed preaching expedition accomplished,
why should it encourage us to bear sufferings? There is
no hope or encouragement for us in thinking that Christ's
sufferings were followed by a preaching expedition into
Hades, when we do not know the results of that preaching. This doctrine does not fit into the context of the
passage, as required by question (3) above.

THE TRUE INTERPRETATION OF I PETER 3:19

Naturally we are unsatisfied to say, "I don't believe that Christ
went to hell." We want to know what we may believe as truth.
It seems to us that the true interpretation of I Peter 3:19 may be
perceived from what has been written before in this special study,
and from these verses:

(1) I Peter 1:11 — "The prophets - - - prophesied - - -
searching what manner of time the *Spirit of Christ,
which was in them,* did signify, when it *testified* before-
hand the sufferings of Christ."
(2) II Peter 2:5 — Noah was "a preacher of righteousness."
(3) Genesis 6:3 — "And the Lord said, My *Spirit* shall not
strive with man forever, for that he also is flesh."

God's Spirit, which is the same as the Spirit of Christ, or the
Holy Spirit (Romans 8:9), strove with men in the days of Noah.
But it was through the prophets (preachers) that the Spirit of
Christ testified. Noah was a preacher of righteousness. In the
days of Noah, Christ's Spirit preached through Noah to those who
were disobedient in those days, and who have therefore ever since
been reserved in prison unto judgment. And, of course, they were
in prison when Peter wrote his epistle.

Let us test this interpretation in the light of the three questions
given before:

(1) There is nothing in this interpretation out of harmony
with the exact words and thoughts of the text (I Peter
3:19).

(2) This view is in harmony with the Scriptures given above (I Peter 1:11; II Peter 2:5; Genesis 6:3). A parallel thought is in Ephesians 2:17. In that passage Paul told the Ephesians that Christ *came and preached peace to you that were far off.* Of course, Christ came and preached to the Ephesians in the persons of His apostles, just as He went and preached in Noah's day through Noah. In both cases, the Spirit of Christ preached, but the words were uttered through human lips.

(3) This interpretation fits wonderfully into the context of the passage, which is designed to teach us that we should suffer, if need be, for well doing, because Christ so suffered. Note how well it fits into the argument:

Peter mentioned (3:18) that Christ's Spirit was quickened after His sufferings. Having mentioned Christ's Spirit, he said that ALSO Christ went in that Spirit and preached to the spirits now in prison. Of course, that preaching was done long before He suffered. Note that FEW (only eight) were saved as a result of that preaching.

Since that time Christ has suffered and died to bring us unto God. He wished to bring the men in Noah's day to God, but few obeyed.

Behold now the increased power in the preaching of Christ since His sufferings. Millions of souls have been saved through water (baptism), while only eight were saved through water in the days of Noah before Christ suffered. Those who read Peter's letter could themselves testify that Christ's preaching to them through His apostles was vastly more fruitful than His preaching in old times through Noah before He suffered.

According to I Peter 3:21, we are saved by baptism through the resurrection of Christ. If there had been no suffering, there would have been no resurrection. With no resurrection, there would have been no baptism and no salvation. Christ's sufferings were therefore necessary and very fruitful. We should take courage by the example of His sufferings.

Christ once said (John 12:32), "And I, *IF* I be lifted up from the earth (that is, crucified), will draw all men unto me." This increased spiritual power of Christ to draw all mankind since His suffering, is what Peter meant by Christ being *quickened in spirit*.

What about the other Scriptures that are set forth as support for the doctrine that Christ went into Hades?

(1) Ephesians 4:8-9. — See the notes in this book on these verses.

(2) Matthew 27:52-53 — We know nothing whatsoever about this event, except the bare facts as recorded. It is pure speculation to try to make these verses fit into a theory about Christ going into Hades. The temporary resurrection of these saints is no greater a miracle than the resurrection of Lazarus and similar events. Many things occurred during the earthly sojourn of Christ that proved His deity. This event certainly proved that Christ was the very Son of God. More we cannot say.

(3) I Peter 4:6 — Who are *the dead* to whom the gospel was preached? They were not the souls of the dead, but those who were once alive, and are now dead. When they were living, the Word of God was preached to them. Now they are dead. Thus the gospel was preached to the dead. This verse should help us to understand I Peter 3:19, which tells of Christ preaching to the spirits *in prison*.

I Peter 4:5, the verse immediately preceding the one we are now considering, speaks of Christ as being ready to judge the quick (or living) and the *dead*. This obviously refers to those who will have died before Christ returns, as contrasted to those who will be living when He comes back.

Our conclusion is that the doctrine that Christ went into Hades is not taught in the Bible, and contradicts the Bible. It is an unprofitable, speculative, controversial, confusing teaching. A man could hold this doctrine and still be a Christian, but the doctrine itself is error.

ANCIENT
The inner port, the market-plac